£5

THE
WINCHESTER
BIBLE

P R E V A
R I C A
T V S.
E
S
T.
M O
A B

misit: postquam mortuus est achab.
Ceciditq; ochozias p cancello cenaculi
sui quod habebat in samaria. & egrota
uit: misitq; nuntios dicens ad eos: Ite
consulite beelzebub dm accaron: utru
uiuere queam de infirmitate mea hac.
Angelus aute dni locutus est ad helia
thesbiten dicens: Surge ascende in
occursum nuntiorum regis samarie.
& dices ad eos: Numquid non est df
misrl: ut eatis ad consulendu beelze
bub dm accaron? Quam obrem hec
dicit dns: De lectulo sup que ascen
disti non descendes: sed morte morieris.
Et abiit helias: Reuersiq; sunt nun
tii ad ochozia. Qui dixit eis: Qua
re reuersi estis? At illi responderunt
ei: Vir occurrit nobis. & dixit ad nos.
Ite & reuertimini ad regem qui misit
uos. & dicetis ei: Hec dicit dns: Num
quid non erat dns in isrl: quia mittis
ut consulatur beelzebub df accaron?
Iccirco de lectulo sup que ascendisti
non descendes: sed morte morieris.
Qui dixit eis: Cuius figure & habi
tus est uir qui occurrit uob: & lo
cutus est uerba hec? At illi dixe
runt: Vir pilosus: & zona pelli
cia accinctus renibus. Qui ait: Heli
as thesbites est. Misitq; ad eum quinquagena
rium principem. & quinquaginta qui erant
sub eo. Qui ascendit ad eum: sedentiq; in uertice
montis ait: Homo dei rex p cepit ut descendas.
Respondensq; helias dixit quinquagenario:
Si homo dei sum: descendat ignis de celo. & dé
uoret te & quinquaginta tuos. Descendit itaq;
ignis de celo. & deuorauit eum. & quinquagin
ta qui erant cum eo. Rursum misit ad eum prin
cipem quinquagenarium alterum. & quinqua
ginta cum eo. Qui locutus est illi: Homo dei

hec dicit rex: Festina descende. Respondens
helias ait: Si homo dei ego sum: descendat ignis
de celo. & deuoret te & quinquaginta tuos. De
scendit ergo ignis de celo. & deuorauit illum. &
quinquaginta eius. Iterum misit principem
quinquagenarium tertium. & quinquaginta
qui erant cum eo. Qui cum uenisset: curuauit
genua contra heliam. & precatus est eum & ait.
homo dei: noli despicere animam meam. &
animas seruorum tuorum qui mecum sunt. Ecce
descendit ignis de celo. & deuorauit duos prin
cipes quinquagenarios primos. & quinquage
nos qui cum eis erant: sed nunc obsecro: ut mise
rearis anime meę. Locutus est autem angls dni
ad heliam dicens: Descende cum eo: ne timeas.
Surrexit igitur: & descendit cum eo ad regem.
& locutus est ei: Hec dicit dns: Quia misisti nun
tios ad consulendum beelzebub dm accaron:
quasi non sit ds in isrl a quo possis interrogare
sermonem: ideo de lectulo sup que ascendisti
non descendes: sed morte morieris. II.

Mortuus est ergo iuxta sermone dni que locu
tus est helias. & regnauit ioram frater eius
p eo: anno seco ioram filii iosafath regis iude: n
enim habebat filium. Reliqua autem uerbou
ochozie: que opatus est: nonne hec scripta sunt
in libro sermonum dierum regum isrl? Factu
est autem cum leuare uellet dns heliam p turbine
in celum: ibant helias & heliseus de galgalis.
Dixitq; helias ad heliseum: Sede hic: quia dns
misit me usq; bethel. Cui ait heliseus: Viuit dns
& uiuit anima tua: quia non derelinquam te.
Cumq; descendissent bethel: egressi sunt filii
prophetarum qui erant in bethel ad heliseu:
& dixerunt ei: Numquid nosti quia hodie dns
tollat dnm tuum a te? Qui respondit: Et ego
noui: silete. Dixit autem helias ad heliseum:
Sede hic: quia dns misit me in iericho. Et
ille ait: Viuit dominus & uiuit anima tua: qa
non derelinquam te. Cumq; uenissent iericho:
accesserunt filii prophetaru qui erant in iericho
ad heliseum. & dixerunt ei: Numquid nosti qa
hodie dns tollat dnm tuum a te? Et ille: Et
ego noui: silete. Dixit autem ei helias: Sede hic:
quia dns misit me ad iordanem. Qui ait:
Viuit dns & uiuit anima tua: quia non dere
linquam te. Ierunt igitur ambo pariter. &
quinquaginta uiri de filiis pphetaru secuti sunt
qui & steterunt e contra longe. Illi autem ambo
stabant sup iordanem. Tulitq; helias pallium
suum. & inuoluit illud. & percussit aquas: que
diuise sunt in utramq; partem. & transierunt
ambo p siccum. Cumq; transissent: helias dixit
ad heliseum: Postula quod uis ut faciam tibi

THE WINCHESTER BIBLE

Claire Donovan

THE BRITISH LIBRARY

WINCHESTER CATHEDRAL

To my mother, a constant inspiration, with love

Author's note This study, published 900 years after the consecration of the Cathedral, offers an introduction to the Winchester Bible to the general reader, and particularly to the visitor to the Cathedral Library where it is displayed. Only four openings of this great Bible can be seen at one time, but, as this book shows, many more illuminations lie hidden. The book is in two parts. In the first section, illustrated in full colour, the manuscript is set in its historical context, setting out its origins and the processes by which it was made. The second section follows through the whole Bible, from its prefaces to the apocalypse, considering the text, the illustration and the style, enabling the reader to experience the manuscript as a whole. Biblical quotations are taken from a translation of the Latin Vulgate (*The Holy Bible*, (Douay Version, Douay AD 1607: Rheims AD 1582), London 1955), but the unfamiliar uses of names of persons and of books are changed, and cited according to the King James Bible. For example, the Vulgate uses Kings. Books 1 to 4, where books 1 and 2 are known in the King James' as the books of Samuel. Similarly, Abdias is Obadiah, Anna is Hannah, Nebuchodonosor is Nebuchadnezzar. Reading the script (where it is shown in the illustrations) reveals the Vulgate spelling of the Winchester Bible scribe.

Many have helped my research, most vitally John Hardacre, librarian and curator at Winchester Cathedral, without whose unfailing generosity in providing access to the Bible the work would never have been begun. The project would have got nowhere without the enthusiasm of the Dean, the Very Reverend Trevor Beeson, and David Way, my editor, of the British Library. I thank also William Voelkle and Roger Wieck of the Pierpont Morgan Library, New York, who gave me access to the Morgan Leaf. The importance and the quality of the new colour photography is obvious, and I thank Miki Slingsby for his painstaking perfectionism and his care, and for his good company during many hours of cramped work. I have gained from the ideas and advice of many, who will recognise these thanks, but for constant support, encouragement and brisk criticism I thank, as always, Colin Platt.

Publishers' Note In this book, all illuminated initials are reproduced at approximately half actual size. Full pages are reproduced at slightly less than half actual size. Other illustrations are reproduced at varying sizes.

© 1993 Claire Donovan

Illustrations of the Winchester Bible are reproduced by permission of the Dean and Chapter of Winchester Cathedral. Illustrations of the Morgan Leaf are reproduced by permission of the Pierpont Morgan Library, New York.

First published 1993
jointly by The British Library, Great Russell Street, London WC1B 3DG and Winchester Cathedral Enterprises Ltd., 5 The Close, Winchester, Hampshire SO23 9LS

British Library Cataloguing in Publication Data is available from The British Library

ISBN 0 7123 0303 0

Designed by James Shurmer

Typeset in Linotron 300 Bembo by Bexhill Phototypesetters, Bexhill on Sea

Printed in England by BAS Printers Ltd, Over Wallop

(*Front cover*) The Book of Jeremiah: Jeremiah receives his prophecy from God (f. 148); *Master of the Leaping Figures*

1 (*Half title*) The Book of Wisdom: Solomon and the prophets accept the book from the wise man (f. 272v); *Master of the Leaping Figures*

2 (*Frontispiece*) The second book of Kings (4 Kings): Elijah consulted by the messengers of Ahaziar, taken up in the chariot of fire, casts his mantle to Elisha (f. 120v); *Master of the Leaping Figures*

3 (*Title page*) The Book of Genesis: detail of the seventh medallion, Christ of the Last Judgement enthroned on the double rainbow with the Cross of Life (f. 5); *Master of the Genesis Initial*

(*Back cover*) The Book of Ezra, f. 342, *Master of the Apocrypha Drawings*

THE WINCHESTER BIBLE

The significance of the Winchester Bible is plain to see. No visitor to the library of Winchester Cathedral can fail to be impressed by its importance. To the visitor of today, used to bibles printed in tiny letters on thin paper as a single handy-sized book, the Winchester Bible's four huge volumes state emphatically that this is the most important text of all. The size and regularity of the script speak of the care with which it was written. The gold and colour of the great illuminated initials which begin each book proclaim the no-expense-spared lavishness of the patron. The artists of these initials made good use of the generous space provided for their part of the enterprise to furnish a visual introduction to the theme of each book, from Genesis to Apocalypse. The quality of their work is among the very best illumination of its time, executed between *c.*1160 and *c.*1175 within the cathedral priory.

Fig.29

Few manuscripts of the cathedral priory survived the Reformation of the sixteenth century. The Bible is first mentioned in the 1622 catalogue of those which remained in the cathedral Library. It was recorded then as a two-volume bible. Apart from a few years when it was taken from the Library during the Civil War, and a period during the 1939–45 war when it was removed for safety, the Bible has always been kept in Winchester. Even the twelfth-century story of a bible from Winchester being lent to St Hugh, prior of the Carthusian monastery of Witham, seems to refer to another great bible – the one now in the Bodleian Library in Oxford. Only since the Bible has become a celebrity have volumes been lent for exhibition, most recently to the London exhibition *English Romanesque Art, 1066–1200* in 1984. The 'Morgan Leaf' was exhibited there too, but this had already been shown alongside the Bible in 1936, when it was displayed in Winchester, on loan from the Pierpont Morgan Library, New York. This leaf, one of the great masterpieces of Romanesque illumination, has long been recognised as having been designed for the Bible but there is little doubt that for much of its existence it was in fact bound into the Bible, an essential part of its illustration.

The Winchester Bible is the biggest of the surviving twelfth-century bibles made in England, with a page size of approximately 583 × 396mm. (23 × 15¾ ins). The 468 folios of calf-skin parchment are remarkably even and smooth in texture for pages so big. The variations in colour are mostly due to the way they have been used over the succeeding centuries – some folios more thumbed than others, some evidently left standing open, causing discolouration of the pale creamy parchment. Openings which start a new text with the grandest historiated initials are the most darkened – evidence of the importance of this as a Bible for display.

Despite this the Bible is in astonishingly fresh condition. It handles like an object of today, not some dusty relic of the past. Its freshness starts with the binding. Its most recent binding was in 1948 when the Dean and Chapter commissioned Beatrice Forder

4 (*Opposite*) The second Book of Samuel (2 Kings): The death of Saul, the grief of David and the killing of the Amalekite (f.99v); *Amalekite Master over a design of the Master of the Leaping Figures*

to rebind the manuscript from the three volumes into which the original two volumes had been divided in 1820. Miss Forder recreated the original division at the opening of the Psalter to form the start of the new Volume 3 on folio 218. She sub-divided this at the end of a quire, towards the end of the fourth Book of Kings, to start the new Volume 2 with the end of that text on folio 129. The new Volume 4 begins with the Book of Judith, although the chapter headings for Judith are left behind, ending the last quire of Volume 3. Each quire was resewn, and each volume given new parchment fly-leaves and mounted between pale oak boards, set with cream leather spines, tooled in gold. The leaves were not trimmed and they retain the gilt edges of the nineteenth-century binding. The Bible has probably been bound only three times – its original binding into two volumes, its second binding into three volumes in 1820 (the leather-covered boards survive), and the third into the present four volumes.

The text of the Winchester Bible is complete, fully written by a single scribe (with only few interventions by another), but the elaborate programme of illustration planned to historiate the initials of its text, and the three (possibly four) full pages of imagery, were left incomplete, the unfinished designs for initials apparently waiting for the illuminator's return. Although 48 of the major initials standing at the beginning of a text are completed, many others are left unfinished at all stages – simply as spaces left by the scribe, outline sketches, inked drawings, drawings with gold applied, even a few which are fully gilded and painted with colour washes but which lack the finishing details of drapery modelling or facial features. And among those completed historiated initials many are the work of two hands, a designing artist working in one style, being painted over by another in a quite different style – altering the movement of figures, the flow of drapery, the detail of facial features and eyes. As a result, the study of the Winchester Bible provides a guided tour of the many processes of production of such an elaborate manuscript, uncompromisingly described by Walter Oakeshott as the best: 'During the twelfth century a series of magnificently large Bibles was produced in England, of which the Winchester Bible is the finest.'

Walter Oakeshott's work on the Bible and its artists occupied him for many years. It was Oakeshott who securely identified the various illuminators in the Bible, distinguishing the one from the other by the way they designed, drew, applied gold and painted the historiated and the decorative initials. It was Oakeshott who gave them their inspired names – the Master of the Leaping Figures, the Master of the Apocrypha Drawings, the Master of the Morgan Leaf, the Amalekite Master, the Genesis Master, the Gothic Majesty Master. It was Oakeshott who noted the frequent occurrence of one artist designing an initial to be completed by another. New work on the illumination of the Bible must always start with Oakeshott.

It was Oakeshott also who identified the initial to Obadiah as that cut from the Winchester Bible. This, one of the nine illuminated initials to have been cut out, was purchased from its private owner by the National Art Collections Fund to be resewn in place in 1948 (fig.24). Although the date 1626, written in the margin next to the hole where once was the initial to Deuteronomy on f.57, suggests that these losses happened

Fig.50

5 (*Opposite*) The Book of Genesis: The Creation of Eve, the Flood, the sacrifice of Isaac, Moses given the tablets of the Law, the anointing of David, the Nativity, the Last Judgement and the resurrection of souls (f.5); *Master of the Genesis Initial*

INCIPIT
LIBER GE
NESIS:
N PRIN
CIPIO CRE
AVIT DEVS
CELET ERRA

Terra autem erat inanis &
uacua · & tenebre erant
sup faciem abyssi · & sps
dei ferebatur sup aquas ·
Dixitq; dr̄ · Fiat lux · Et
facta est lux · Et uidit dr̄
lucem quod ēt bona · &
diuisit dr̄ lucē atenebris ·
Appellauitq; lucē diē · &
tenebras noctē · Factūq;
est uespe & mane · dies un̄
Dixit quoq; dr̄ · Fiat firma · II
mentum inmedio aquarū ·
& diuidat aquas abaquis ·
Et fecit dr̄ firmamentū ·
diuisitq; aquas que erāt
sub firmamento · ab iis
que erant sup firmamtū ·
Et factum est ita · Voca
uitq; dr̄ firmamentū cē
lum · & factū est uespe &
mane · dies secundus ·
Dixit uero dr̄ · Congre · III
gentur aque que sub
celo sunt inlocū unum ·
& appareat arida · Fac
tūmq; est ita · Et uocauit
dr̄ aridam terrā · congre
gationesq; aquarū appel
lauit maria · Et uidit dr̄
quod ēt bonum · & ait · Germinet terra herbā
uirentē & facientē semen · & lignū pomiferum
faciens fructum iuxta genus suū · cuius semen
insemetipso sit sup terram · Et factū est ita ·

Et protulit terra herbam uirentem · & ferentem
semen iuxta genus suum · lignumq; faciens
fructum · & habens unū quodq; sementē sedm
speciem suam · Et uidit dr̄ quod ēt bonū · fac
tumq; est uespe & mane · dies tertius · .IIII.
Dixit aute dr̄ · Fiant luminaria · infirma
mento celi · & diuidant diem & noctem ·
& sint insigna & tempora · & dies & annos · & lu
ceant infirmamento celi · & inluminent tiram ·
Et factum est ita · Fecitque dr̄ duo magna lu
minaria · Luminare maius ut preēt diei · &
luminare minus ut preēt nocti · Et stellas ·
Et posuit eas infirmamento celi · ut lucerent
sup terrā · & preessent diei ac nocti · & diuiderent
lucem actenebras · Et uidit dr̄ quod ēt bonū ·
& factū est uespe & mane · dies quartus · .V.
Dixit etiam dr̄ · Producant aque reptile
animē uiuentis · & uolatile sup terram ·
sub firmamento celi · Creauitq; dr̄ cēte gran
dia · & omnē animā uiuentem atq; motabi
lem · quā pduxerant aquē inspecies suas · &
omne uolatile sedm genus suum · Et uidit
dr̄ quod esset bonum · benedixitq; eis dicens ·
Crescite & multiplicamini · & replete aquas
maris · auesq; multiplicent sup terrā · Et fac
tum est uespe & mane · dies quintus · VI.
Dixit quoq; dr̄ · Producat terra animā ui
uentem ingenere suo · iumenta & reptilia
& bestias terre sedm species suas · Factumq; est
ita · Et fecit dr̄ bestias terre iuxta species suas ·
& iumenta & omne reptile terre ingenere suo ·
Et uidit dr̄ quod ēt bonum · & ait · Faciam
hominem ad imaginē & similitudinē nr̄am ·
& preēt piscibus maris & uolatilib; celi · &
bestiis · uniuersēq; terre · omniq; reptili
qd mouetur interra · Et creauit dr̄ hominē
ad imaginē suam · ad imaginem dei creauit
illum · masculum & feminā · creauit cos · Be
nedixitq; illis dr̄ · & ait · Crescite & multiplica
mini · & replete terram · & subicite eam · & domi
namini piscibus maris & uolatilib; celi · & uni
uersis animantib; que mouentur sup terram ·
Dixitq; dr̄ · Ecce dedi uob omne herbā afferen
tem semen sup terram · & uniuersa ligna que
habent insemetipsis sementē generis sui ·
ut sint uob inescam · & cunctis animantib; tr̄e
omniq; uolucri celi · & uniuersis que mouentur
interra · & inquib; est anima uiuens · ut ha
beant ad uescendum · Et factum est ita · Vi
ditq; dr̄ cuncta que fecit · & erant ualde bo
na · Et factum est uespe & mane dies sixtus · VII
Igitur pfecti sunt celi & terra · & omnis ornatus
eorum · Compleuitq; deus die septimo op
suum quod fecerat · & requieuit die septimo ·

5

long ago, it seems that some of these initials were cut out in more recent times. Perhaps they still survive. Some whole folios have also been cut out, and it is not impossible that miniatures on single folios (like the Morgan Leaf) might also have been removed. It is to be hoped that further fragments from the Bible may re-emerge, and that this study of the Bible might help their present owners to identify their origins.

The illumination and decoration of the Bible dominates the theme of this book, but it also endeavours to offer a sense of the Bible in the context of the community of monks for which it was made and the patron whose project this was. In the second part of the book (pp.34–63) the whole process of production, the layout and the writing, the subject matter as well as the style of the illumination, is set out by examination of the Bible from beginning to end, Genesis to Apocalypse.

THE BIBLE AND THE MONKS OF WINCHESTER

For the community of monks which served the Cathedral Priory of Saints Peter and Paul and Saint Swithun in Winchester, the bible was central to their lives. It was the quarry from which the texts of the daily life of the monastery were extracted. Each part of their day – which began in the early hours of the morning, well before the dawn – was dominated by readings from and interpretation of the bible, both the Old and the New Testament, structuring the liturgy and the office, framing and guiding the discussion of the community in Chapter, and providing intellectual and spiritual sustenance during meal-times. The main texts of the daily liturgy and divine office, the psalms, lessons, gospels and epistles, which they recited and sang in choir, were drawn from the bible. Indeed, the culture of medieval monastic life was fundamentally biblical; the literary, musical and artistic life of the community was created through the spiritual life, which was dominated by the bible.

Of the community of St Swithun's, the Benedictines of the Old Minster of Winchester, there would have been at least sixty monks, maybe as many as eighty, in the later twelfth century. The daily routine of the community, as was the case for all black monks, was set out initially in the Rule of St Benedict, although modified and elaborated over the succeeding centuries of monastic life. This way of life, the *Opus Dei*, regulated each hour of the day, to be occupied by prayer, work or reading. The reading, the *lectio divina*, was essentially scriptural, including biblical texts set out with a gloss or glosses to guide the reader's understanding; the scriptures explained, inter-related and compared. The monks' reading also included the works of the doctors of the church, among them Jerome, Augustine, Gregory and Ambrose, and the study of biblical commentaries, the work of generations of biblical scholars, from Origen to Jerome, Augustine to Abelard. The *lectio divina*, together with the needs of the liturgy and choir, created a demand for books, prominent among them biblical texts. For many of these purposes there was no need for a complete bible, and many manuscripts containing only single texts or sections of the Old or New Testaments were written – workaday copies for daily use. Gospel books, glossed bibles, volumes of the epistles, psalters, lectionaries (containing 'lessons' drawn from both Old and New Testaments), and apocalypse (the revelation of St John), all would have been required, and each kept in the most appropriate part of the priory buildings, in the choir, chapels, vestry, cloister, refectory and chapter house. But for the great monasteries of the twelfth century (some of which, like Winchester, were cathedrals as well) a complete bible had become a vital possession.

When Lanfranc arrived in England in 1070 to be the new Norman archbishop of Canterbury, he brought with him a scholar's respect for an accurate text of scripture, mingled with the churchman's yearning for uniformity of practice. The complications of the bible text, its various versions and translations, had given an exceptional level of importance to the 'correct' text. The notion of the 'authorised' version, the translation accepted as the 'truth', was as important to the twelfth-century reader as to one of the twentieth century. Lanfranc was insistent that all monastic foundations in England should have a Vulgate bible, with a text which agreed as nearly as possible with those of the monasteries of the Continent – particularly the Benedictine foundations of Normandy, like Bec where Lanfranc had been educated. This insistence, together with the ambitions of the communities, is reflected in the survival of large-format twelfth-century bibles from many of the major monasteries. The making of a bible at the abbey of Bury St Edmunds (Suffolk), one volume of which survives (Corpus Christi College, Cam-

6 Psalm 1: David kills the lion and the bear, Christ releases the boy possessed by the Devil and the souls from torment in the Harrowing of Hell (f.218); *Master of the Genesis Initial over a design of the Master of the Leaping Figures*

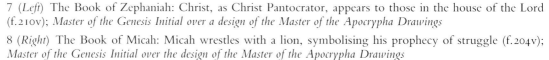

7 (*Left*) The Book of Zephaniah: Christ, as Christ Pantocrator, appears to those in the house of the Lord (f.210v); *Master of the Genesis Initial over a design of the Master of the Apocrypha Drawings*

8 (*Right*) The Book of Micah: Micah wrestles with a lion, symbolising his prophecy of struggle (f.204v); *Master of the Genesis Initial over the design of the Master of the Apocrypha Drawings*

bridge), is recorded in *c.*1135–8. Of a similar date and scale is the Lambeth Bible, perhaps from Canterbury (two volumes, in Lambeth Palace Library and Maidstone Public Library, Kent). In the library of Durham Cathedral one large bible from the beginning of the twelfth century (the Carilef Bible) is surpassed in size by a bible of the end of the century which was given to Durham Cathedral by Bishop Hugh du Puiset. Most of the important monastic foundations would, by the mid-twelfth century, have had at least one complete and large-scale bible with a carefully copied text, taken from an exemplar believed to be correct. But even when an exemplar was found from which a true text could be copied, mistakes, grammatical errors and misspellings were inevitable, and the effort to present a reliable text is often evident in the corrections, instructions, additions, each set into the margins of their huge pages. Although these bibles differed from one another in the fine detail of translation and interpretation, and even in more fundamental matters such as the order in which the books were written, they were all based on the Vulgate, the compilation originally made by St Jerome, used throughout the medieval Western church.

The importance of St Jerome as the bible's translator and commentator is acknowledged in the Winchester Bible, as in most twelfth-century vulgates, through the prologues which prefix each book and contribute to the authority of the bible. The Winchester Bible was not a scholar's bible, but it was a complete text of the Vulgate, including the Old and New Testaments, two versions of the psalms, the apocrypha, the epistles and the apocalypse of St John. And it needed a theological setting of the words to satisfy its monastic audience, and to emphasise the continuity of biblical truth from the early church and the earliest communities of Christians.

A complete bible – a pandect – was an essential part of the furnishings of so great a cathedral priory as St Swithun's, a compendium of all the texts required for the life of its community which were otherwise scattered about the monastic buildings. Its significance was emphasised by its huge size. Originally bound in two volumes, each volume would have comprised well over 200 folios of calf-skin parchment. Lying open, each volume is some 600mm. (2ft) high by 800mm. (2ft 8ins) in span. It is a bible for display, designed to be read while standing at a lectern. While it would have been moved from place to place, between the priory buildings and the cathedral, if it truly belonged to the community (and not the bishop), its 'home' lectern may well have been in the chapter house, the community's private space, where regular readings of scripture took place. Its large and even script is readily legible, and the gold and colours of the illuminated initials would have shone across such a space, enabling the community to share its illustration. Its physical presence lends weight to the truth of the text, a vital attribute of twelfth-century lectern bibles. But it was also a bible for ceremony. To carry this bible open in procession on the great feasts of the liturgical year would have required the determined efforts of two well-grown novices – no task for a boy. The ceremonial attached to the reading of the bible – kissing the sacred text, showing the opened pages Fig.29 to the listeners, even the simple act of turning a page – is made ever more solemn with a bible so big and so richly illuminated. Scriptural knowledge, spiritual understanding, praise, worship and beauty are all brought together in this Bible.

ST JEROME AND THE MEDIEVAL BIBLE

The bible text in use in the Middle Ages was known as the Vulgate, the 'common', which had been generally agreed to comprise the 'canonical' or approved texts in the eighth century. However, the scholarship of St Jerome in the fourth century had been central to the establishment of this canon, and his identification with the Vulgate was much stronger in the Middle Ages than it is today.

Jerome's early studies of the classics and of rhetoric had provided him with a scholarly approach to editing texts so that, on returning to Rome in *c.*382 from years of travel, he

9 (*Left*) The Book of Ezechiel: The Vision of Ezechiel, who sleeps by the river Chobar, of the tetramorph symbolic of the evangelists with the feet of a calf; and of the interlocking wheels full of eyes (f.172); *Master of the Morgan Leaf*

10 (*Right*) The Prayer of Habbakuk: Habbakuk prays, led to 'high places singing psalms' by the Lord (f.208); *Master of the Morgan Leaf*

readily took up the commission of Pope Damasus to edit and revise the old Latin texts of the four New Testament gospels. Jerome re-translated them from the Greek, chiefly from the texts which had been compiled by Origen, a scholar of Alexandria, who had created a degree of order from the conflicting scriptural texts. However, Jerome recognised that any Latin translation drawn from the Greek remained at a distance from the 'Hebrew truth'. And, exceeding his commission from Damasus, he began a study of Hebrew from which his translations established a standard in biblical scholarship which merited the confidence of generations of churchmen who relied on the Vulgate.

Jerome translated the gospels, and then turned to the psalter. Of his three editions, the Romanorum has remained in continuous use in the Vatican; the Hebraeorum, a translation directly from Hebrew, was much appreciated as the most authentic; but his third version, the Gallican, was the one which became the psalter text of the Vulgate bible. Even so, double, even triple, versions of the psalters were written into bibles in the Middle Ages, most often, it seems, the Gallican and the Romanorum versions, although in the Winchester Bible the Hebraeorum is set next to the Gallican.

Searching for the origins of the scriptures and theological truth, Jerome travelled to Bethlehem in 384 where he revised all the Old Testament books then accepted as canonical by Hebrew scholars. As he did so he wrote a prologue for each book, which established its place in the Christian canon and set the biblical text into Jerome's own exegetical framework, explaining it through his personal interpretation and making cross-references to other parts of the bible. Further writings on the bible survive in Jerome's considerable correspondence, including a letter to Paulinus of Nola, which sets out each of the Old Testament books and provides a summary of Jerome's symbolic commentary. His advice to Paulinus was entirely relevant to the medieval reader of the bible, advising caution when interpreting the scriptures. In the compilation of the Vulgate as made from the ninth to the twelfth centuries, some of these letters were frequently included, together with the prologues to the various books. As in the Winchester Bible, the Vulgate often opens with Jerome's letter to Paulinus of Nola, with a letter to Pope Desiderius standing as a preface to the Old Testament, and a letter to Pope Damasus, written while still a relatively young man, as a preface to the New Testament. The inclusion of these prologues and prefaces contributes to the authority of

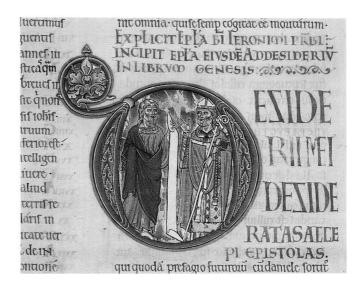

11 St Jerome's letter to Desiderius: St Jerome with Pope Desiderius, who is vested as a medieval bishop, as Bishop Henry, the Bible beneath his arm (f.3); *Master of the Genesis Initial*

the bible. In the Winchester Bible they are given visual authority by the way in which each is set out with a large painted initial, the *incipit* and opening words set out in display script.

Jerome's personality and scholarly activity were well-known to the medieval audience of the Vulgate. His exegesis of the biblical text went beyond these prologues, and his works were part of the prescribed reading of the Benedictine communities. They would also have known his etymological interpretation of the proper names found in scripture (*Liber de nominibus hebraicis*) and a gazetteer-like compilation of the geography of the bible (*Liber de situ et nominibus locorum hebraicorum*). The importance of St Jerome went beyond the bible, to the interpretation of history and symbol, and to moral exhortation and encyclopaedic science.

The Vulgate was used throughout the Western church until the Reformation in northern Europe, and it is still used in the Roman Catholic church to this day. However, its standardisation was in no way complete by the twelfth century, and the efforts then of much biblical scholarship, in particular those of Archbishop Lanfranc, had been devoted to ensuring that as correct a text as possible was in use in the Benedictine foundations of England. This version, inevitably, looked back to the origins of the Vulgate and to St Jerome, as twelfth-century biblical scholars attached just as much importance to the tracing of the text to its origins as had Jerome.

THE PATRONAGE OF HENRY OF BLOIS

There is no record that states conclusively who was the patron of the Winchester Bible. Yet the layout of the manuscript and its script date to *c.*1160, when Henry of Blois was bishop of Winchester, just when, after a life-time of travel and public activity, he turned Fig.11 to a more contemplative life in his diocese. A portrait of a bishop, grandly arrayed and with a red volume beneath his arm in a historiated initial at the very beginning of the Winchester Bible, surely confirms his importance to the considerable undertaking this manuscript represents. Money given by Henry to the cathedral scriptorium in 1170, shortly before his death, may have been partly to hasten the completion of this Bible. And perhaps the fact that it was never completed was a consequence of his death.

Bishop Henry was not unused to large undertakings. Among the great bishops of the twelfth century, few left their diocese with more substantial reasons to remember them than did Henry of Blois, bishop of Winchester (1129–71). After his early years, brought up in the great monastery of Cluny in southern France, Henry arrived in England in 1126, to be placed by Henry I as abbot of Glastonbury Abbey in Somerset. Although he remained their abbot until his death in 1171, little of his life was truly dedicated to the affairs of the monks of Glastonbury. But he did build for them. He created great abbey buildings, including buildings for the monks and palatial buildings for himself – which he rarely occupied. As bishop of Winchester, his building energies were also first focused on a palace for himself. Work to enlarge and improve Wolvesey Palace, overlooking the walls of the Cathedral Close, was undertaken soon after his arrival and continued to receive attention through much of his forty-two years as bishop.

His interests in the arts were clearly those of a lavish-spending patron, and his tastes developed through frequent travels in Britain and Europe on his many ecclesiastical and

12 (*Left*) The Book of Leviticus: The punishment of Korah, Dathan and Abiram for their challenge to Moses and Aaron, swallowed by the earth (f.34v); *Master of the Genesis Initial*

13 (*Right*) The Book of Joshua: God's command to Joshua to pass over the Jordan with the people and his assembly of the 'princes of the people' (f.69); *Amalekite Master over a design of the Master of the Leaping Figures*

political ventures. He was often in France, with visits to Cluny taking him towards the south, where many great building projects were under way, including the series of pilgrimage churches on the way to Santiago de Compostella. He also visited Rome, where, in common with many contemporary visitors, he learnt to appreciate the antique buildings of the city, and the classical statuary still freely to be seen. It was probably on a visit in 1151, when he was summoned by the pope to answer allegations made against him by Bernard of Clairvaux (who was his constant critic), that his enthusiasm for antique art was recorded. John of Salisbury wrote of Bishop Henry's purchase of statues, presumably to adorn his palace of Wolvesey, which he then shipped back to Winchester, stopping on his way to visit the shrine of St James at Compostella.

Bishop Henry's Tournai marble fonts, his church at East Meon, his hospital at St Cross, and his castle-palaces at Wolvesey, Farnham and Bishop's Waltham show him to have been the most active of patrons. So also do a pair of enamel plaques with inscriptions which identify Bishop Henry as donor and patron. Around the portrait of *Henricus episcop'* the inscription includes: 'Henry, alive in bronze, gives gifts to God'. He is represented prostrate in prayer clutching his crozier and a great tablet, an altar of decorative marble, like the cosmati work of medieval Rome. The second plaque depicts a pair of censing angels, and is enclosed by an inscription which recalls the mid-century turmoil of the wars between Stephen and Matilda. The inscription translates '. . . may the angel take the giver to heaven, after his gifts, but not just yet, lest England groan for it, since on him depends for peace or war, agitation or rest': something of an over-estimate of Henry's true contribution to peace. In 1141 Bishop Henry briefly turned from the support of his brother, King Stephen, in his dispute for the throne with the Empress

Matilda, daughter of Henry I. But, switching allegiances again, he was subjected to a siege brought by Matilda which inflicted great destruction on Winchester. Those fine enamel plaques, which evoke these turbulent times, must once have adorned some fine liturgical object, maybe the altar itself or a chalice to be placed upon it, probably made in Winchester although they are ascribed to the hand of a Mosan enamelist of great skill.

There is evidence of many craftsmen in Winchester at this time, including foreigners such as marble sculptors from Tournai in the 1160s, and of Henry's many donations to the cathedral, including metalwork vessels and liturgical objects. Much of the surviving work of the artists in Winchester remains as tantalising fragments like these enamel plaques, some pieces of sculptural decoration, and only a tiny representation of the illumination, including those of the Winchester Bible.

The library in Winchester Cathedral has long been dispersed, leaving only a handful of manuscripts from this period, but some survive in other libraries, including a second bible and a gospel book, both now in the Bodleian Library, and an illustrated psalter of *c.*1150 in the British Library. The connections between this psalter, St Swithun's, and Bishop Henry are strong, as indicated by the prayers to St Swithun and the Cluniac feasts in its calendar. Among the many miniatures of purely English inspiration, some of which look back to iconographic traditions of Anglo-Saxon Winchester, are two full-page miniatures of the Assumption and the Enthronement of the Virgin, apparently copied from a Byzantine icon. Henry's enthusiasm for Byzantine work was shared with many of Europe's greatest patrons of art in the second half of the twelfth century, and his travels were at a time when many Byzantine-inspired fresco cycles and mosaics were being completed – in particular the mosaics of Cefalu Cathedral and of the Capella Palatina in Palermo, Sicily. In his psalter the copied 'icon' provides certain evidence of his enthusiasm for Byzantine work, in addition to his taste for the antique. And the Byzantine-inspired work in the Winchester Bible, the gessoed gold grounds shimmering like the gold backgrounds to the mosaics of Sicily and Rome, further suggests his influence on its style. But whereas the writings and correspondence of Abbot Suger, Bishop Henry's near contemporary, establish the scale and influence of his patronage of the arts, Henry's correspondence has not survived. Yet his influence on mid-twelfth-century Winchester could hardly have been less than that which Abbot Suger ascribes to himself at St-Denis.

MAKING THE BIBLE

The scriptorium at St Swithun's Priory in the twelfth century was undoubtedly a busy place. This was not new. For centuries manuscripts had been written and illuminated in this scriptorium to serve the needs of the monastery and its bishops. In the Life of St Hugh of Lincoln, written by Adam of Eynsham shortly after the saint's death in 1200, the existence of two fine bibles belonging to St Swithun's, Winchester is revealed. The story tells how the king, Henry II, had persuaded the prior of St Swithun's to release a bible for the Carthusians of Witham, of which Hugh was then prior. The bible Hugh received was described as complete and carefully corrected. When Hugh later discovered from a visiting Winchester monk that it had not been the king's bible to give, he insisted on its return, and refused to consider the offer of an even bigger bible from Winchester,

which was described as shortly to be finished. The bible lent to Witham must have been the two-volume vulgate from the cathedral priory which is recorded as given to the Bodleian Library in Oxford by a canon of the cathedral in 1601. This bible (Bodleian MS Auct. inf 1–2) is complete, carefully corrected and finely decorated with illuminated, but not historiated, initials throughout. Whether it was actually written and illuminated in the cathedral priory scriptorium has been questioned. But textual details show that it was certainly at Winchester undergoing modifications – the addition and correction of text, the completion of decoration – at the time when the Winchester Bible was being worked on.

This work on the Winchester Bible was never completed, and only hints of the intended illustration and decoration of the New Testament survive in the drawn designs for initials. Yet the amount of labour already expended was phenomenal. There is little doubt that this Bible was the great project of the priory scriptorium from about 1160, although it is written by just one scribe, with only minor additions and corrections by another. While it has been calculated that the writing of such a manuscript represents the work of some four years or so, this huge enterprise would have occupied space in the scriptorium for longer than this while the coloured initials and display script were added. Evidence of style suggests that work on the illumination continued over a much longer period, perhaps as long as fifteen years. And still it was left unfinished.

The text however is complete, written on 468 folios of fine quality, calf-parchment, identifiable by the pattern of veins which is visible on some folios. As each bifolium measures more than 583 × 792mm. (23 × 31¼ins), an entire calf-skin would have been used for each one, and the Bible must have used the skins of some 250 calves. The elaborate processes of the preparation of parchment – the scraping, treatment with lime, the stretching, the drying and the washing – represent many hours of labour in the production, and the parchment alone represented a great expense. This parchment would have been bought from the professional parchment makers of Winchester, whose products would have been much in demand for the making of books in the various monasteries and nunneries in the city, and also for the many charters and other documents required for the government and business of the city and the diocese.

The prepared parchment, laid flesh-side to flesh-side, hair-side to hair-side, into quires of four bifolia, needed to be ruled. To make sure each folio presented an identical size and shape of text – the hallmark of the presentation of a well 'published' text – each quire of eight folios was pricked through to mark out and guide the ruling. The pattern of ruling is consistent throughout the Winchester Bible, forming a text space of 54 lines in two columns set in a constant margin. The guide pricking may be seen on the outer edge Fig. 30 of most quires, only some quires retaining the pricking for the eight vertical rulings, mostly trimmed away during binding. Guide lines scored into the surface of the parchment in dry-point joined pricking to pricking, both groove and ridge being equally effective as a guide for the scribe. Only a single bifolium differs. This, ff.131 and 134, Fig. 16 is written on identical parchment which had been already ruled in dry-point. However, these 'supply' leaves were written by a different scribe, who preferred a page ruled in pen – dry-point ruling was becoming old-fashioned from the mid-twelfth century. This

14 (*Opposite*) The Book of Judith: the full-page drawing stands as a preface to the book of Judith, and depicts her conquest of the army of Holofernes (f.331v); *unfinished, Master of the Apocrypha Drawings*

Non auerraf faciem tuam ame inquacumq: die   Ne abfcondaf faciemtuam ame indic tribulatio

15 Psalm 101: The Angel of Death slays David's people in punishment for numbering the people and, the Angel's hand stayed, he offers a sacrifice in atonement (f.246); *unfinished, Master of the Morgan Leaf over a design by the Master of the Leaping Figures*

scribe also corrected the text of the Bible, and he completed the text of Malachi on ff.213v–214, inexplicably left unfinished.

Otherwise, the text of the Winchester Bible was written entirely by a single scribe who maintained his regular and even hand throughout the task, the smooth rounded contours of the miniscules sitting low on the scored ruling. As both ascenders and descenders of these letters are short, a distinct and precisely measured interval is left between each of the lines, with only single line capitals, abbreviation marks, and accents for stress or emphasis to help the reader, appearing in the upper portion of each line space. This stately script is characteristic of mid-twelfth-century monastic manuscripts, developed from the Carolingian-derived scripts of tenth-century English monasteries and influenced by continental writing imported with the influx of Norman monks and monastic houses in the late eleventh century. This scribe was surely a monk of the priory, and the rather old-fashioned characteristics of both the script and the ruling format might be expected of the head of the scriptorium, trained in the traditions of some years before.

This role may have been taken by the precentor, whose responsibilities included ensuring that books were available for the needs of the community. He, with other experienced scribes, would have trained young scribes to write, to lay out a text, and to

16 (*Opposite*) The Book of Isaiah: The prophet Isaiah receives the prophecy from the Lord on a scroll (f.131); *Master of the Gothic Majesty*

ISIO.
YSA
IE.FI
LIA
MOS
QVĀ.

VIDIT. SVP. IVDÃ. G. IERLM.
iy diebus Ozie Ioatham Achaz et Ezechie
regum iuda. Audite celi. & auribz pcipe ter
ram: quam dñs locutus est. Filios enutriui
& exaltaui. ipsi autem spreuerunt me. Cog
nouit bos possessorem suum: & asinus presepe
domini sui. isrl autem me non cognouit: poplus
mis non intellexit. Ue genti peccatrici poplo
grati iniquitate. semini nequam. filiis scelera
tis. Dereliquerunt dñm. blasphemauerunt
scm isrl: ab alienati sunt retrorsum. Sup quo
peuiam uos ultra addentes preuaricationem.
Omne caput languidum. & omne cor merens.
A planta pedis usq; ad uerticem: non est in eo
sanitas. Uulnus & liuor. & plaga tumens non
est circumligata. nec curata medicamine: neq; fo
ta oleo. Terra ura deserta: ciuitate ure succense ig
ni. Regionem uram coram uobis alieni deuo
rant: & desolabitur sicut in uastitate hostili.
Et derelinquetur filia syon ut umbraculum
in uinea. & sicut tugurium in cucumerario:
sicut ciuitas que uastatur. Nisi dominus
exercituum reliquisset nobis semen: quasi
sodoma fuissemus. & quasi gomorra similes
essemus. Audite uerbum domini prin
cipes sodomorum: percipite auribus legem
dei nostri populus gomorre. Quo michi
multitudinem uictimarum urarum dicit
dominus. Plenus sum. Holocausta arie
tum & adipem pinguium: & sanguinem
uitulorum & agnorum & hircorum nolui.
Cum ueneritis ante conspectum meum: qs
quesiuit hec de manibus uestris: ut ambu
laretis in atriis meis. Ne afferatis ultra sa
crificium frustra: incensum abominatio est
michi. Neomeniam & sabbatum & festiui
tates alias non feram: iniqui sunt cetus uri.
Kalendas uestras & solennitates uestras

INCIPIT. LI
BER.YSA
IE. PROPHE.

paint display letters and flourished initials. These novices would have been engaged in other tasks too – in the preparation of parchment ready for the scribe, maintaining the quality of the pens and the sharpness of the knives, preparing the ink and the paints, and ensuring that the exemplar for copying was provided straight and adequately lit.

Writing – copying – was an important part of the *Opus Dei*, and time for such work was set aside during the hours of the morning, after the regular meeting of Chapter, which followed the office of Terce. Members of the community were expected to take their part in the many writing duties which, in a substantial land-owning priory such as Winchester, included the preparation of property transactions, inventories and charters, quite apart from the service books for the use of the community and copies of texts for the library. The greatest writing expertise was still at this time held within the monasteries, although already, in the latter part of the century, there are records to show that professional scribes were engaged by some monasteries, hired as one of the many servants attached to the larger houses. While there is no surviving record of hired scribes working for St Swithun's, the location of the priory in the city of Winchester, where much court and government business was transacted employing scribes, would have ensured that professional assistance with writing for the business needs of the priory would have been readily available locally.

To find an examplar for a correct bible text might have been a more difficult task. And, as the story of the bible lent to St Hugh illustrates, the scriptorium might well have used an exemplar on loan from another Benedictine monastery. The close textual links between the Winchester and the Bodleian Bibles certainly shows how important was this matter of a correct text in the writing of a bible. Although the Bible was written with great care for accuracy in the first place, there are a number of different levels of correction within it. Sometimes the scribe has himself discovered an error, and has erased and replaced it in its correct place on the line, easily detectable because the roughened

Fig. 30

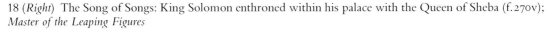

17 (*Left*) The Book of Exodus: The young Moses slays the Egyptian in retribution for the tormenting of the Hebrew (f.21v); *Master of the Leaping Figures*

18 (*Right*) The Song of Songs: King Solomon enthroned within his palace with the Queen of Sheba (f.270v); *Master of the Leaping Figures*

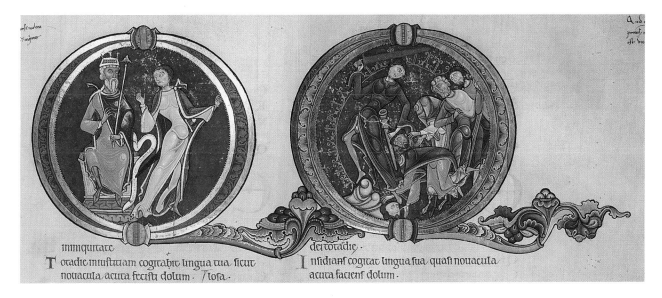

inmiquitate
confirmatione
singuone
dei totadie

T otadie miustiuam cogitabit lingua tua, sicut
nouacula acuta fecisti dolum. / Iosa.

I nsidians cogitat lingua sua, quasi nouacula
acuta faciens dolum.

19 Psalm 51: Saul urges his servant Doeg to slay Ahimelech the priest and his companions, loyal to David
(f.232); *Master of the Leaping Figures*

surface of the parchment absorbs the ink differently. But sometimes the correction is
written in the margin, its place in the text noted with insertion marks. Both these types
of correction depend upon the diligence of the scribe cross-checking his own work, and
are corrections simply of mis-copying, not of variant readings of the text.

The correctness of the Bible did not depend solely on this scribe, as further corrections
were undertaken by the scribe of the replaced bifolium of ff.131 and 134. He, writing
only slightly later than the first, endeavours to make his sections blend smoothly into
the whole, copying the size and disposition of the letters. But his script is different; it is
more spiky than the main script, more 'gothic' in style. Where the main scribe corrected   Fig.16
only to insert omissions or to alter misreadings, this second scribe often supplies small
sections of an alternative reading interpolated neatly in the margin. These alternatives do
not appear beyond the end of the psalter section. Yet the quire numbers (at the base of   Fig.2
the final verso of each quire throughout the original first volume, in the centre of the
first recto of each quire in volume two) are written in his hand also, which suggests that
he continued to be involved until the unfinished Bible was bound. This scribe has been
identified as the corrector also of the Bodleian Bible, and the texts of the two bibles have
been modified to conform. These two great bibles must once have been together in the
scriptorium at Winchester, lying open at the identical page, while the scribal editor pored
over the two, comparing, correcting, completing.

Marks left by the craftsmen at each stage of the making of the Bible are still visible:
the text for the rubricator, colour instructions for the painted initials, instructions to the   Fig.69
illuminator, marks identifying the folio sequence within the quires. These instructions,
which would have been erased had the manuscript ever been truly finished, reveal the
mechanics of the enterprise. The layout of the Winchester Bible has a consistent hierarchy   Fig.22
which determines the correct level of decoration for each text, with appropriate spaces
for initials, rubrics and display script set out by the scribe. Each new text of the Bible,
whether a minor prologue of St Jerome, of only a dozen or so lines, or a major biblical
book, opens with an *'incipit'* (the title identifying the text) and closes with an *'explicit'*
(identifying the text just completed). The display script, in coloured paints of red, blue

20 Prologue to the Minor Prophets: A tanglewood decorative initial inhabited by beasts dominated by a blue centaur which, facing Hosea, forms a fine opening (f.197v); *Master of the Morgan Leaf over a design by the Master of the Apocrypha Drawings*

and green, is mostly in 'squared' capitals, usually tall straight-backed capitals, the work of a number of rubricators, probably monastic scribes. Sometimes the letters are embellished with decorative infills (Joel, f.200v), or are stacked intricately one inside the other like Celtic calligraphy (Genesis, f.5, or Ecclesiasticus, f.278v). Display letters of a different style, found only in the original first volume, are sophisticated uncial-type letters in rich blue and red paint. Always consistent both in their form and in the balance of their placement, whether inserted into the shape of an historiated initial (Joshua, f.69) or given ample free space (Isaiah, f.131), these letters may have been supplied by an illuminator rather than a scribe. The squared capitals are found throughout the Bible, including the display lettering in Volume 4, where only one major initial is fully gilded and painted. Earlier in the Bible, where the display script includes both squared capitals and uncial letters, some major complete historiated initials have been overlooked by the rubricator, and entirely lack the display text – a perfect illuminated initial without the text to start the reader off. Perhaps most notably, of the four sets of psalm initials, none

Fig.48
Fig.5
Fig.23
Fig.13
Fig.16
Fig.17
Fig.18

includes the first verse of the text. Psalm 51 has the first words added in the margin by
the secondary scribe; the others leave the reader without help.

The making of the unfinished Winchester Bible reveals a process constantly open to
revision. No logical sequence of processes emerges from the initial preparation of the
parchment to finally handing it to the binder. Nor is there a logical sequence to the
completion of the illumination, although the first volume (of the original binding) was
completed, and the latter part of the second volume remained in the drawn state only –
with some initials left simply as spaces. Even so, the Winchester Bible has 46 complete
and fully illuminated initials in gold and colours, most of them historiated. Eighteen
further historiated initials are substantially drawn, some of them also gilded. And eight
huge holes show where once were yet more illuminations. Four full-page miniatures –
the two fully painted sides of the Morgan Leaf and the two full-page drawings for Judith
and Maccabees – survive from a programme of miniature painting which very likely
included a full-page miniature facing the opening of the psalms, now cut out, and three

Fig.19

Fig.53

Fig.27

Fig.14

Fig.71

pages of canon tables preceding the gospels, which would have been elaborately decorated, although probably left only as drawings.

Yet, with all this richness of quantity, the Bible is best known for the quality of its illumination. It is this which has been most written about. Thanks to the names given by Walter Oakeshott to the illuminators of this manuscript, they have acquired personalities. The Master of the Leaping Figures conjures in the imagination just the style that we see – figures brilliantly coloured, leaping and writhing. The Master of the Apocrypha Drawings was also a painter, and his drawings were only a preliminary. Yet his name directs attention to the exquisite surety of his line – a linear, two-dimensional style, his figures gently poised on delicately drawn tiptoes. These two artists work in the characteristic style of the mid-century; the form of the figures stylised into patterns of limbs and drapery, enriched with gilded edges. They apply gold leaf flat on the surface of the parchment, the uneven surface showing through the burnished layer of gold. Despite similarities, these two are easily distinguished from one another in the drawn state – the Apocrypha Master's clear outline contrasting with the patterning and infilling of the Leaping Figures Master – and through their quite distinct palettes. Whereas the Leaping Figures Master's style is like other Winchester work, that of the Apocrypha Master has been related to the abbey of St Alban's, a community where many manuscripts were being made, and which had contacts with Bishop Henry.

Like this artist, the work of the four illuminators whose styles draw on the mixture of classical and Byzantine inspiration of the end of the century, gives every indication of travelling professionals, taking on a variety of projects as required. Through Walter Oakeshott's publication of the Sigena Chapter House paintings in Catalonia, all-but destroyed in the Spanish Civil War, some of these artists of the Bible are envisaged as European travellers: yesterday Palermo, today Winchester, tomorrow Barcelona. Similarities between the decorative work of the Genesis Master (Winchester acanthus enfolded and elaborated) and decorative work at Sigena, bring these two enterprises close together. His figures, robust and strongly modelled, are parallelled in the narratives of Sigena. The quiet figures of the Gothic Majesty Master also find echoes at Sigena, the Isaiah of the Bible tellingly set next to a Sigena shepherd in Oakeshott's book, whereas the Morgan Master's solemnity, the green-modelled faces and thick curling beards, forge links with the almost contemporary mosaics of Sicily. His work is also linked with Sigena, in particular with the portrait-like heads of the ancestors of Christ. The image of the monastic artist labouring in the confined cloister of Winchester Cathedral through the whole of a life of prayer, is exploded by the widely travelled Masters of the Morgan Leaf and the Genesis Initial.

Yet the Morgan Master's style is translated into wall-paintings within Winchester Cathedral itself, in the Holy Sepulchre Chapel. The painting of the Deposition and Entombment of Christ on the east wall of this small chapel demonstrates many features of his style: the firm outline, the green underpainting, the fall of the drapery, the expressive seriousness of the poses and faces. The palette, its strong red and blue comparable to the richness of the verso of the Morgan Leaf, contrasts markedly with the

22 (*Opposite*) The Prayer of Jeremiah and the Book of Baruch: The white-haired prophet Jeremiah sends his prayer to God above. The prophet Baruch reads his book of prophecy to the people of Babylonia (f.169); *Master of the Morgan Leaf*

noster·completi sunt dies nostri·qa uenit finis noster·
Uelociores fuerunt psecutores nostri COPh.
aquilis celi·sup montes psecuti sunt nos· in
deserto insidiati sunt nobis· 5 ubus· REX.
Spu oris nostri xpc dns captus est in peccatis
nostris cui diximus· in umbra tua uiuem ingen
Gaude & letare filia edom qui ba SEN
bitas interra bus· ad te quoq; pueniet calix
inebriaberis atq; nudaberis· TAV
Completa est iniquitas tua filia syon·non
addet ultra ut transmigret te·Visitauit ini
quitate tua filia edom· discooprit peccata tua
FINIT LAMENTATIO IEREMIE·Pphe.

IN CIPIT ORATIO EIVSDEM :

ECORDARE
dne quid acciderit nob
intuere & respice op
probrium nostrum·
Hereditas nostra uersa
est ad alienos· domus
nostre ad extraneos·
Pupilli facti sumus
absq; patre·matres
nostre quasi uidue·

Aquam nostram pecunia bibimus· & ligna
na nostra precio comparauimus·
Ceruicibus minabamur lassis
non dabatur requies·
Egypto dedimus manum & assyrius·
ut saturaremur pane·
Patres nostri peccauerunt & non sunt·
& nos iniquitates eorum portauimus·
Serui dominati sunt nostri· & non fuit
qui nos redimeret de manu eorum·
in animabus nostris afferebamus panem
nob a facie gladii in deserto·
Pellis nostra quasi clibanus exusta est
a facie tempestatum famis·
Mulieres in syon humiliauerunt·
uirgines in ciuitatibus iuda·
Principes manu suspensi sunt· facies
senum non erubuerunt·
Adolescentibus impudice abusi sunt·
& pueri in ligno corruerunt·
Senes de portis defecerunt· iuuenes
de choro psallentium·
Defecit gaudium cordis nostri· uersus est in luc
tum chorus noster·cecidit corona capitis nostri·
ue nobis quia peccauimus·
Propterea mestum factum est cor nostrum· ideo
contenebrati sunt oculi nostri·
Propter montem syon quia disperiit·

uulpes ambulauerunt in eo·
Tu autem dne in eternum pmanebis· solium tuum
in generatione & generationem·
Quare imperpetuum obliuisceris nostri· & dere
linques nos in longitudinem dierum?
Conuerte nos dne ad te conuertemur· IN
noua dies nostros sicut aprincipio·
Sed piciens reppulisti nos·iratus es contra
nos uehementer· FINIT ORATIO IEREMIE:

INCIPIT·PROLOGVS·IN·LIBRV·
BARVCH·NOTARII·IEREMIE·Pphe·

Liber iste qui baruch nomine pnotatur· in hebreo
canone non habetur· sed tantum inuulgata editione· Si
militer & epla ieremie·pphete· Propter notitiam autem
legentium hic scripta sunt· quia multa· de xpo nouissimisq;
temporibus indicas·

DINIT PROLOGVS

De oratione & sacrificio pro uita Nabuchodonosor·

INCIPIVNT LIBRI BARVCH·ET EPISTOLA IEREMIE
PROPHE:

ET·
VERBA
LIBRI
QVE SCRI
PSIT

baruch filius neeri· filii amasie· filii sedechie·
filii sedei· filii helchie· in babylonia· in anno
quinto· in septima die mensis· in tempore quo
ceperunt chaldei ierlm & succenderunt eam igni·
Et legit baruch uerba libri huius ad aures ie
chonie filii ioachim regis iuda· & ad aures uni
uersi populi uenientis ad librum· & ad aures
potentium filiorum regum· & ad aures presbi
terorum· & ad aures populi a minimo usq;
ad maximum eorum· omnium habitantium in
babylonia· ad flumen sudi· Qui audientes
plorabant· & ieiunabant· & orabant incon
spectu dni· Et collegerunt pecuniam secdm
quod potuit uniuscuiusq; manus· & miser
int in ierlm ad ioachim filium helchie filii salon
sacerdotem· & ad reliquos sacerdotes· & ad
omnem populum qui inuentus est cum eo in ierlm·

25

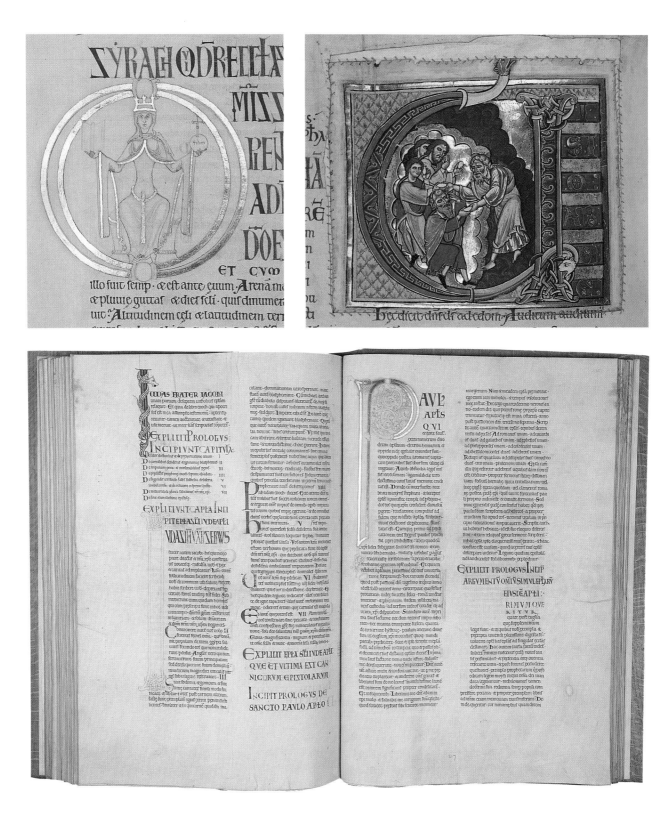

23 (*Top, left*) Ecclesiasticus: The drawing complete with gilding of the enthroned figure of Wisdom who holds the sceptre of faith and the book of Wisdom (f.278v); *Master of the Leaping Figures*

24 (*Top, right*) The Book of Obadiah: Resewn into the Bible, the initial shows Obadiah, steward to King Achab, taking food to the hiding prophets (f.203v); *Master of the Genesis Initial over a design by the Master of the Leaping Figures*

25 (*Above*) Epistle of St Jude (f.434v); Prologue to Epistles of St Paul (f.435); *unfinished Master of the Leaping Figures*

26 (*Opposite*) The Book of Proverbs: The enthroned crowned Solomon passes the scroll of his parables, wisdom to the wise man, knowledge and understanding to the young man (f.260); *Master of the Gothic Majesty over a design by the Master of the Leaping Figures*

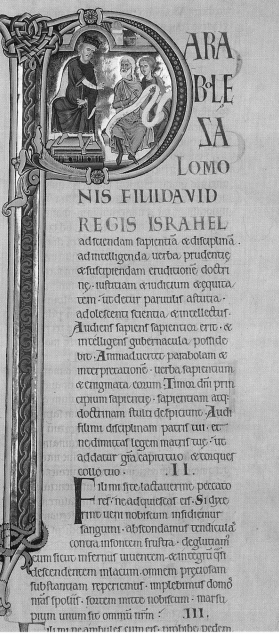

paler pigments of the later layer of wall-painting which overlaid this scheme in the early thirteenth century. How far an artist turned his hand to different forms of painting is difficult to assess, although there is plenty of positive evidence that some artists at least worked in a wide range of media and the close stylistic parallels with the Bible provide ample evidence of the wall painting and the illumination progressing together, hand in hand. And undoubtedly, just as only a glimpse remains of the quantity of contemporary manuscript illumination, this painted chapel provides only a token of the amount of wall-painting that once overlaid the walls of the cathedral and priory buildings.

The collaboration between the artists is complex and paradoxical. Yet the evidence is rich. The styles in which the illuminators worked are distinct and readily distinguished one from another, even on those occasions when two work on the same initial. The stylistic differences are fundamental, not a matter of handling or small stylistic quirks

Fig.18
Fig.12
Fig.41
Fig.13

alone. In comparing the work of the Master of the Leaping Figures at his most elegant and sinuous (Songs of Songs, f.270v) with the robust vigour of the Genesis Master (Leviticus, f.34v), or the solemnity of the Morgan Master (Prayer of Jeremiah, f.169) with the fussy fragility of the Amalekite Master (Joshua, f.69), the fact of their inclusion in this single manuscript requires an explanation which recognises these artists as professionals, employed by the priory scriptorium, but having developed their styles through contact with a variety of artistic centres. Were these artists not all found in this same book, they would each have been ascribed to quite different centres of production, and their work dated some twenty years apart. By this date it is already difficult to identify the place in which an illuminator was working by means of his painting style; often it is a question of tracing the movements of professional artists, who worked in different places, moving from job to job. And dating the work of such professionals is less precise than their static counterparts. The diversity of style as seen in this manuscript, with clear evidence of shared work, complicates dating by style: complicates even the dating of work within the manuscript itself, where the evidence often indicates collaboration between the most diverse of artists.

Without doubt, the Winchester Bible was not intended to end up as it has. Its illumination was intended, surely, to parallel the precision of the script, to echo the impression of the carefully edited text. Such rich contemporary manuscripts as the Bury or Lambeth Bibles, or the sister manuscript of the Winchester Bible, the Bodleian Bible, demonstrate a single purpose of design and illumination. While in the Bodleian Bible the main illuminator (named the Master of the Entangled Figures) is accompanied by another (the Brilliant Pupil), the name given to this second – while perhaps not precisely defining the relationship – indicates that the illustration looks similar throughout. As in the Winchester Bible the secondary scribe tried to write like the main scribe, so in the Bodleian Bible the Brilliant Pupil's painted initials were intended to look like those of the Entangled Figures Master. Moreover, although other unfinished manuscripts survive from this period (as all others), the intended design usually shows at the start, providing a model for the completed whole. The first few quires at least demonstrate the intention. This is not the case with the Winchester Bible. The first illuminated initials of the Bible are the work of the Genesis Master, in a later style than the Master of the Leaping Figures, whose hand does not appear until the fourth initial of the Bible, and whose greatest sequence of work is in the final volume.

Even so, good reasons have identified the Master of the Leaping Figures as the primary designer of the Bible, and the unfinished drawings in the final volume are his. Many more completed (painted and gilded) initials were designed by him, although over-painted by others. He was an artist of supreme imagination and consummate skill, and his work can be said with confidence to date to the period suggested by the script. He at least was contemporary with the scribe, and with Bishop Henry. So, why does the Leaping Figures Master not start the illustration, with Genesis at least? And why, if he was so close to the scribe, did he sometimes design an initial which filled only part of the space left available by the scribe, or overfilled the space so as to exclude the display

27 (*Opposite*) The Morgan Leaf: the recto includes the *capitulae* to the first Book of Kings and depicts episodes of the life of Samuel and the anointing of Saul (Pierpont Morgan Library MS 619); *Master of the Morgan Leaf over a design of the Master of the Apocrypha Drawings*

1. De ionathe & dauid amore & de odiu saul in dauid. &
ubi in centu pputiis philistinox accepit michol filia sa
ul uxore que patris dolu pdens saluum fecit dauid.

2. De fuga dauid ad samuelem. & quomodo q̃ missi fuerant
ut eu raperent pphetauerunt ubi & saul ipse ueniens pro
phetauit. & de pacto ac signo ionathe & dauid q̃d in mu
cem piisserunt. Transiit ad regem moab.

3. De fuga dauid in nobee. & de his que abimelech sacerdote
facta esse referunt. & quomodo saul immutauit uultu
suu coram achis rege geth & collabebat & cu suis omnib;

4. De gad ppha ubi comonuit dauid fugere in terram iuda. in sal
tum sareth a facie dauid. & doech pdente occisus est abimelech
reliquis octoginta sacerdotib; & quomodo dauid piissit phi
listium & saluauit ceila.

5. De saule quomodo uoluit dauid in ceila capere. qui con fugi
ens uenit in desertum ziph. ubi ionathan ad eum uenit. &
piissit uterq; fedus coram dño. & confortauit ionathas da
uid. & reuersus est in domum suam.

6. De dauid in spelunca procidit coram clamidis saul silenter.
& piissit cor suum dixitq; ad uiros suos. propicius sit m dñs
ne mittã manum mea in dñm meu rege. quia xp̃c dñi est.

7. De samuelis morte & sepulchro eius in ramatha. & que de
nabal carmelo ac de abigail uxore eius gesta referuntur.

8. De dauid ubi abigail & achinoem uxores accepit. & ubi sau
lis psequentis scyphum & hastam abstulit. eiq; scdo pe
percit. Iterem cor i suluit. Occubuit.

9. De transfugio dauid in geth ad achis regem philistin &
que illic gesserit. & de Saule quomodo pphitonissam mu

10. De philisteis aduersus Saul congregatis ad monte in bello
gelboe. & de dauid ubi piissit amalech omne captiuitatem
& uxores suas reduxit in siceleg. dixeruntq; hec est preda dauid.

11. De bello philistinox in monte gelboe. in quo saul cum trib; filiis

29

28 The Morgan Leaf: the verso is fully painted and depicts episodes in the life of David: his conquest of Goliath, his survival of Saul's attempt to kill him through jealousy, his anointing as king by Samuel, and the death of Absalom, mourned by David (Pierpont Morgan Library MS 619); *Master of the Morgan Leaf over a design of the Master of the Apocrypha Drawings*

29 1 Samuel, The first Book of Kings: Elkanah at dinner with his wives, Penninah and Hannah, who weeps for a child; while below she sings her canticle of thanksgiving for Samuel (f.88); *Master of the Morgan Leaf over a design of the Master of the Apocrypha Drawings*

script, as for Exodus (f.21v)? And why, if he was the artist most closely involved at the design stage, is it so often his illuminated initials that lack the opening letters of the text?

The Winchester Bible both informs and continues to challenge notions about the making of an illuminated manuscript. In this enterprise an aesthetic adventure unfolds, with the early style superseded by the later, designs over-painted and fundamentally modified. Even the primary importance of the historiated initial is challenged by the introduction of the full-page miniatures, only one of which was ultimately brought to completion, and that by a later-style artist. Where the early style draws on the essentially English style of manuscript illumination, the group of travelling artists who descended on Winchester possibly as early as 1170 to complete the work, brought in an unmistakable breath of foreign air – Byzantine and inspired by large-scale wall decoration. The determination of the patron may be discerned behind their arrival.

The decision to include full-page miniatures after the layout of the text had been done is evident from changes to the physical structure – the collation – of the manuscript. Evidence survives that at least two insertions were made, in both cases to include a full-page miniature. In one case that miniature, to the book of Judith, remains (f.331v). Another, the Morgan Leaf, has since been removed. But at other points the evidence of the collation reveals losses, leaves cut out. A leaf is missing from the very beginning of the original second volume, facing the opening of the psalter on f.218, which was removed after the original binding as the quire number is lost with it. Three leaves, presumably the canon tables, have been cut out from the start of the gospels, ff.372–4.

Fig.14

INCIP. EPLA. BEATI. IHERONIMI. AD PAV LINV. PRBRM. DE STV DIO. DIVINARR. SCPTVRARR.

RATER AMBRO SIVS TVA MI THI MVNVCVLA PERFERENS.

detulit & suauissimas litteras: que in
principio allocutionis fidem pbate
iam fidei & ueteris amicitie pfere
bant. Vera enim illa necessitudo est
in xpi glutino copulata: qua non ut
litas rei familiaris. non presentia tan
tum corporum. non subdola & pal
pans adulatio. sed dni timor & diui
narum scripturarum studia concili
ant. Legimus in ueteribus hystoriis
quosdam lustrasse puincias: nouos
adisse populos. maria transisse. ut
eos quos ex libris nouerant. corā quoq;
uiderent. Sic phitagoras memphiticos
uates. sic plato egyptum & architam
tarentinum. eandeq; horam italie que
quondam magna grecia dicebatur.
laboriosissime pagrauit: ut qui athe
nis magister erat & potens. cuiusq;
doctrinas achademie gymnasia pso
nabant. fieret peregrinus atq; discpls.
malens aliena uerecunde discere:
qm sua impudenter ingerere. Deniq;
dum litteras quasi toto fugiens or
be psequitur: captus a piratis & ue
nundatus: etiam tiranno crudelissi
mo paruit captiuus. uinctus & ser
uus. & tamen quia philosophus.
maior emente se fuit. Ad titum liuium
lacteo eloquentie fonte manantem. de ulti
mis hispanie galliarumq; finib; quosdam ue
nisse nobiles legimus: & quos ad contemplatio

onem sui roma non traxerat: unius hominis fa
ma pduxit. habuit illa etas inauditum omnib;
seclis celebrandumq; miraculum: ut urbē tanta
ingressi. aliud extra urbem quererent. Apollo
nius siue ille magus ut uulgus loquitur. siue
philosophus ut phitagorici tradunt. intrauit
persas. ptransiuit caucasum. albanos. scithas.
massagetas. opulentissima indie regna penetra
uit. & ad extremum latissimo phison amne
transmisso: puenit ad brachmanas. ut hiarcam
in throno sedentem aureo. & de tantali fonte
potantem. inter paucos discipulos. de natura.
de moribus. ac dierum siderumq; cursu audiret
docentē. Inde p elamitas. babilonios. chaldeos.
medos. assyrios. parchos. syros. phenices. arabes.
palestinos reuersus. ad alexandriam ptexit. per
ethiopiam adiit. ut gymnosophistas & famosissimā
solis mensam uideret in sabulo. Inuenit ille
uir ubiq; quod disceret. ut semp pficiens. semp
se melior fieret. Scripsit super hoc plenissime oc
to uolumnib; phylostratus. Quid loquar
de seculi hominib;: cum apls paulus uas electionis
& magister gentium. qui de conscientia tanti
in se hospitis loquebatur. an experimentum que
ris eius qui in me loquitur xps. post damascū
arabiamq; lustratam ascenderit ierosolimam
ut uideret petrum. & manserit apud eū diebus
quindecim. hoc enim mysterio ebdomadis & ogdoadis
futurus gentium predicator instruendus erat.
rursumq; post annos quatuordecim assumpto
barnaba & tito. exposuerit cum aplis euglium: ne
forte in uacuum curreret aut cucurrisset. ha
bet nescio quid latentis energie uiua uox. &
in aures discipuli de auctoris ore transfusa
fortius sonat. Vnde & eschines cum rhodi exula
ret. & legeretur illa demosthenis oratio. quam
aduersus eum habuerat. mirantibus cunctis
atq; laudantibus. suspirans ait. Quid si ipsa au
dissetis bestiam sua uerba resonantem? Nec
hoc dico quod sit aliquid in me tale. quod
uel possis uel uelis discere: sed quo ardor tuus
& discendi studium. etiam absq; nobis pse proba
ri debeat. Ingenium docile. & sine doctore
laudabile est. Non quid inuenias: sed quid que
ras consideramus. Mollis cera & ad formandū
facilis. etiam si artificis & plastic cesset manus
tamen uirtute totum est. quicquid esse potest.
Paulus apls ad pedes gamalielis legem moysi
& prophetas didicisse se gloriatur: ut armatus
spualib; telis. postea doceret confidenter. Ar
ma enim milicie nre non carnalia sunt. sed po
tentia in dō ad destructionem munitionum. con
silia destruentes. & omnem altitudinem extollente
se aduersus scientiam dei. & captiuantes omnem

The manuscript has been foliated twice, both recently. The first, probably in 1820 when it was rebound, numbered each folio in the centre of the lower margin of each recto, with each of the original two volumes beginning with f.1. This foliation did not include the missing folios. The Bible was refoliated in the top right-hand corner of each recto by Walter Oakeshott, probably at the time of its next re-binding in 1948. He noted the position of removed leaves in pencil notes in the margins, and included them in his foliation. Thus f.371 precedes the three lost folios of canon tables, f.375 is the number given to the next surviving leaf, and Oakeshott noted the losses in the margin of f.371v.

However Oakeshott did not include the Morgan Leaf in his foliation, believing that it had never been inserted. This huge miniature page is now in the Pierpont Morgan Library in New York. It is the only fully painted miniature from the manuscript known to be preserved. With the *capitulae* of 1 Kings and scenes of the life of Samuel on the recto, and a sequence of the life of David on the verso, it is among the greatest pieces of miniature painting surviving from the Romanesque period. Its place was between f.87v and f.88. The continuation of the list of the *capitulae* of 1 Kings is copied onto the Morgan Leaf from f.88, although the layout is slightly different, with the initials set to the left in a separate column, and the red Roman numerals identifying each chapter omitted. There are small textual differences, but these are copyist's errors only. The chapter headings are incorrectly numbered from 1 to 11, obviously after the leaf was removed. Like nearly all the illuminated work in the Bible, it has clusters of small holes through the parchment where silk guards were sewn in to protect the painting at its original binding. As the leaf is painted on both sides these holes are at both top and bottom, the guard to be hinged from the left in each case. This leaf, like the drawing preceding the book of Judith, on f.331v, was inserted into the collation. It could therefore be removed without trace. Scholars have assumed that it was never inserted. However, the marked difference in discolouration on what would have been its two flanking folios, clearly to be seen in fig.29, can only be explained by its presence in place while, over centuries of display as the grandest opening in the Bible, the dust gathered on the surfaces of the verso of the Morgan Leaf and f.88.

The Morgan Leaf is first recorded as being offered for sale to William Morris for £100. He had built up a considerable library of illuminated manuscripts and single leaves, of which there were many in the hands of booksellers at this time – cutting up medieval manuscripts was a popular Victorian pastime. This leaf was too expensive for him, however, and it was ultimately sold to John Pierpont Morgan in 1912 and taken to New York. As a single leaf it was much more vulnerable than as part of a bound book, and the possibility of its separate survival from the twelfth century seems slight. Its condition is good, with only little more abrasion of the gold than is found elsewhere in the Bible. This appearance of the Morgan Leaf on the market at the end of the nineteenth century would fit with a supposition that it was removed at the 1820 rebinding. Perhaps other leaves were removed then, and await rediscovery.

30 (*Opposite*) St Jerome's letter to Paulinus: St Jerome at his desk writes to Paulinus of Nola while Frater Ambrosius, the messenger, awaits the completion of the letter (f.1); *Master of the Genesis Initial*

GENESIS TO APOCALYPSE

Volume 1 (ff. 1–128)

St Jerome's letter to Paulinus, f.1, fig.30

The first text of the Bible opens with four lines of display script, 'INCIPIT EP[isto]LA BEATI IHERONIMI AD PAULINU[s] . . .', 'Here begins the letter of blessed Jerome to Paulinus on the study of the holy scriptures.' The layout of the page is dominated by the historiated initial, the 'F' of 'FRATER AMBROSIUS . . .'. Paulinus of Nola, in search of spiritual truth, corresponded with both the great Doctors of the Church, St Augustine, and St Jerome, then in Bethlehem. Frater Ambrosius, the messenger, had arrived in Bethlehem on pilgrimage to the Holy Land. Jerome's response is full of advice, and he urges Paulinus not to study the sacred scriptures without guidance as, he tells him, the bible is so full of mysteries.

The display letters on this first page are of both types, the *incipit* in blue and red uncial letters, and the red, blue and green square capitals which open the text. The historiated 'F' extends the height of the text column, like a decorative border, interrupted half-way by a medallion enclosing a griffin whose wings are extended to guard the holy text, as did the cherubim before the Holy of Holies (2 Chronicles 5:8). The artist whose work appears first in the Bible is the Genesis Master. His St Jerome, in a composition inspired chiefly by Evangelist portraits, hunches over the writing lectern while Frater Ambrosius waits. The heavily draped figures fill the initial space to overflowing, their faces strongly modelled, with blocks of colour creating heavy brows and deeply set eyes. The burnished gold ground was laid on a fine layer of gesso, revealed where the gold has flaked away. The page is darkened and both the paint and the gold have been badly rubbed. This is evidently a page that has long lain exposed.

St Jerome's letter to Desiderius, f.3, figs. 11 and 31

Jerome's letter to Pope Desiderius stands as prologue to the Old Testament. In the Genesis Master's initial St Jerome and Pope Desiderius fill the space, Jerome even stepping onto the rim of the initial. While Jerome is dressed as a Father of the Church, his letter carried on a rotulus and his cloak draped almost like a toga, Desiderius is vested as a medieval bishop, a gold and

31 St Jerome's letter to Pope Desiderius, f.3, *Master of the Genesis Initial*

white mitre on his head. He is in the guise of Bishop Henry, vested for the grandest of liturgical festivals, 'in copes and in albs', the red-bound book beneath his arm representing the great illuminated Bible to which this initial stands as a preface. The black crosses on his stole may refer to the Hospital of St Cross which Bishop Henry had founded in 1136.

These letters of St Jerome occupy three folios, and the *capitulae* (chapter headings) of Genesis occur on f.4. Folio 4v is left blank, facing the start of Genesis, possibly once intended to be fully illustrated.

The Pentateuch, Genesis to Deuteronomy

These first five books of the Old Testament provide the narratives of the creation, the exile of the Jews, the giving of the Law to Moses and the Covenant to Abraham; and they are typologically equated with the New Testament Gospels.

Genesis, f.5, figs. 3 and 5

The 'I' of *In principio* runs the height of the folio, the decorative terminals overflowing. The square capitals were in place before the initial was painted, although, strangely, the text initials came later and overlap the green edge. Characteristic of the Genesis Master, the initial presses into every fragment of space left by the scribe. The iconography of this initial is full of multiple meanings, as was recommended by St Augustine in his *Confessions*: 'Why should he (Moses) not have had both meanings in mind if both are true? And if others see in the same words a third or a fourth, or any number of true meanings, why should we not believe that Moses saw them all?' (*Confessions*, Book XII, Ch 31). The essence of the meaning is Creation – the start of the text of Genesis. But the seven medallions depict a sequence of events essential to the linking together of scripture – the New Law building on the Old Law, the key to the redemption of Man. The Creation of Eve (Genesis, 1:27 and 2:21–5) leads to sin, and thus to the Flood to wash away the sins of Man (Genesis 6–8). The Sacrifice of Isaac (22:1–19) is the 'type' of the crucifixion; as Abraham at the command of God offers his son in sacrifice, so does God offer His. The Law is given to Moses – both in the stone tablets and the scroll of the covenants (Exodus, 19–34). David's genealogical line leads to Christ (1 Kings, 16:11–13) whose Nativity begins the New Law (St Luke, 2). Christ, displayed in a sarcophagus-like crib, swaddled for sacrifice, sets the theme of this medallion, its multiple meanings of joy and impending sorrow revealed in the faces of Mary and Joseph. In fulfilment of the Old and New Law, Christ presides over the Last Judgement (Apocalypse), enthroned on the double rainbow, the Cross of Life between his knees, recalling his sacrifice and evoking the Trinity. To either side the souls rise from their graves. This sequence of imagery transcends the Creation, as God's design is changed according to circumstance, with forgiveness and new beginnings, to culminate in the redemption and resurrection of souls. In his *Confessions*, St Augustine writes at length on Creation, and he ponders further in his *Exposition of the Literal Meaning of Genesis*. For the monastic community, familiar with Augustine's thought, an iconography such as this was only to be expected. A literal creation narrative for *In principio* would not have done justice to the solemnity of this Bible.

Exodus, f.21v, figs. 17 and 32

In contrast, Exodus is purely narrative. Moses, a Hebrew youth brought up in the court of the Pharaohs, aligns himself with his people, 'In those days after Moses was grown up, he went out to his brethren: and he saw their affliction, and an Egyptian striking one of the Hebrews his brethren. And . . . he slew the Egyptian and hid him in the sand' (Exodus 2:11–12). The jabbing fore-finger of the orange-robed Egyptian signifies his abusive words to the Hebrew. Below, Moses exacts revenge on behalf of his people, and beneath the feet of the falling Egyptian a small pile

32 The Book of Exodus, f.21v, *Master of the Leaping Figures*

of sand represents his burial place. This act of revenge begins the exile of Moses, expelled from Egypt by Pharaoh.

This brilliantly coloured initial is the first in the book illuminated by the Master of the Leaping Figures. In contrast to the Genesis initial, the figures are slender and twisting, draperies clinging damply to the musculature, and flying freely into knots and arrow-headed points. The eyes declare antagonism and revenge, yet the framing is decorative, the initial stems picked out in shone gold, the gold leaf stuck to the parchment with glue and burnished, exposing the roughness of the surface beneath. The rich colour is modelled through darker tones of the same colour, or paler tones which, as in the orange gown of the Egyptian, fade to a white peak where the body's curves culminate. It is stylised elegance of the highest quality, a brush with total security of touch. Yet, the 'H' fills the column width, leaving little space for the missing display script.

Leviticus, f.34v, figs. 12 and 33

The illustration is from the Book of Numbers, the revolt of Korah, Dathan and Abiram, who 'rose up against Moses: and with them two hundred and fifty others of the children of Israel. . .' (Numbers, Chapter 16:2). Moses gathered them together as God commanded him, each with his censer charged (16:16–18). Moses spoke: 'If these men die the common death of men . . . the Lord did not send me. But if the Lord do a new thing, and the earth opening her mouth swallow them down, and all things that belong to them, and they go down alive into hell, you shall

33 The Book of Leviticus, f.34v, *Master of the Genesis Initial*

know that they have blasphemed the Lord.' (16:29–30). The fulfilment of this prophetic speech is depicted; Korah and Dathan represent the two hundred and fifty with censers (16:17), while Moses and Aaron stand aside behind the altar. Then 'the earth broke asunder under their feet; and opening her mouth, devoured them with their tents and with their substance' (16:31–2). 'And a fire coming out from the Lord destroyed the two hundred and fifty men that offered the incense' (16:35).

The Genesis Master sets the scene on a shimmering burnished gold background, the censers also of burnished gold, the pierced detail of the metalwork picked out in black. The contrast between the eager forward strides of Korah and Dathan, and the wild tumbling, head first into the black pit that opens beneath them, is briskly symbolic – swift retribution for rebellion and for pride. Each element expresses the text: the shaft of flickering fire from the glory of the Lord, the depth of the pit – 'the ground closing upon them' (16:33).

Numbers, f.44

The initial to the book of Numbers illustrates an episode from Chapter 21, when Moses in the midst of a plague of 'fiery serpents' sent by the Lord to bite and kill those who spoke against him set up the Brazen Serpent: 'And the Lord said to him, Make a brazen serpent, and set it up for a sign. Whosoever being struck shall look on it shall live. Moses therefore made a brazen serpent and set it up for a sign: which when they that were bitten looked upon, they were healed.'

(Numbers 21:9). This is the Old Testament 'type' of the Crucifixion, and Moses holds aloft a scroll which bears the words of Christ from the Gospel of St John: 'and as Moses lifted up the serpent in the desert, so must the Son of Man be lifted up' (John, 3:4).

Deuteronomy, f.57

The opening 'H' of Deuteronomy is missing. The hole measures 185 × 150mm., but most of the opening display script remains, in square capitals.

Joshua, f.69, figs. 13 and 34

God commanded Joshua, after the death of Moses: 'Moses my servant is dead. Arise, and pass over this Jordan, thou and thy people with thee, into the land which I will give to the children of Israel' (Joshua 1:2). This is the first of the 'two artist initials' in the Bible. The design by the Master of the Leaping Figures is evident both in the poses of the figures and the initial form. Yet the painter, the Amalekite Master, imposes his own style and laid the brilliant gloss of the gessoed gold. The figures no longer leap, the drapery is soft, the faces, underpainted with green, are defined chiefly in line. Like all the soldiers in the Winchester Bible, the armed men of Joshua – the 'princes of the people' (1:10) – are armed as contemporary medieval knights dressed as if for the Crusades. Their round plate helmets have chain mail collars and the shields display heraldic devices, although the different pattern on Joshua's shield in the two registers of the initial suggests

34 The Book of Joshua, f.69, *Amalekite Master over a design of the Master of the Leaping Figures*

that the artist saw this as decoration rather than a device for identification. The recurrent phrase of that first chapter of Joshua, 'Take courage and be strong', must surely have rung true to the generation which saw the loss of Jerusalem to the infidel. Joshua's men declare: 'All that thou hast commanded us we will do: and whithersoever thou shalt send us, we will go.' (1:16). The sentiments echo those of the Crusaders, next to be heard in the summons to the Third Crusade, called by Richard I in 1189.

Judges, f.77v

Judges merited a huge initial. But its 'P', POST MORTEM JOSHUE . . . has been cut out, leaving a hole of 400 × 165mm. (15¾ × 6½ins). The incipit is written by the uncial letters rubricator and, as with Deuteronomy, traces of the green boundary remain on the cut edge.

Ruth, f.85v, fig.35

Ruth opens with an illuminated and gilded initial but without historiation. This 'I' is all the work of the Master of the Morgan Leaf, his first initial in the Bible. The use of gold burnished onto a gesso ground and the twining stems bearing leaves of many colours are characteristic of his decorative style.

The Morgan Leaf, figs. 27 and 28

1 Samuel (1 Kings), f.88, fig.29

When the Bible was first bound, a double-sided miniature – the Morgan Leaf – was inserted to face the initial. These three pages formed an elaborate ensemble, a sequence of narratives to open the books of Kings. It was set out and drawn by the Apocrypha Master and finished by the Morgan Master. These pages provide evidence of the intended elaboration of the illustration introduced after most of the Bible had been laid out. This opening was often chosen to stand open, as is shown by the darkened parchment on f.88 in contrast to the clean surface of f.87v. The loss of this leaf deprived the Bible of its greatest narrative statement.

The narrative starts with the initial, illustrating the opening of the text: 'There was a man of Ramathaim-zophim . . . and his name was Elkanah . . . and he had two wives, Hannah and Peninnah. Peninnah had children, but Hannah had no children. To Peninnah and all her sons and daughters he gave portions, but to Hannah he gave one portion with sorrow, because he loved Hannah.' (1 Samuel (1 Kings) 1:1–5). Depicted at dinner, Hannah weeps for a child.

Hannah's prayers are heard, as the scenes on the

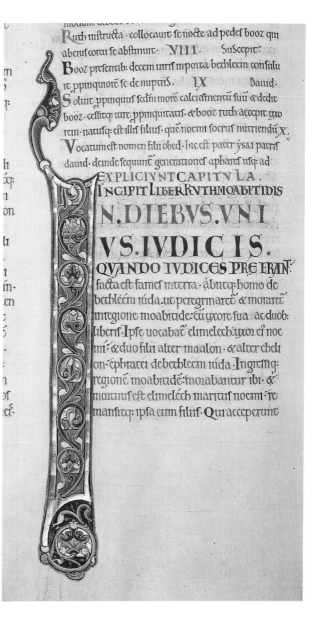

35 The Book of Ruth, f.85v, *Master of the Morgan Leaf*

recto of the Morgan Leaf show, and her child Samuel is dedicated to the Temple, presented to the High Priest Eli, 'And after she had weaned him, she carried him with her, with three calves, and three bushels of flour, and a bottle of wine, and she brought him to the house of the Lord in Shiloh. Now the Child was as yet very young' (1:24). The gifts brought to the Temple with the Child are shown, as the boy is received by Eli.

Hannah rejoices: 'My heart hath rejoiced in the Lord and my horn is exalted in my God: my mouth is enlarged over my enemies, because I have joyed in thy salvation.' (2:1). This, the canticle of Hannah, is one of the great hymns of praise of the liturgy, which would have rung familiarly in the ears of the priory community. Half-way down the stem of the historiated capital

'F', Hannah stands with the scroll carrying the words of the canticle, her face lifted in praise. Taken alone, the story given in the initial is incomplete, needing the scenes from the Morgan Leaf to fill in the detail.

The child Samuel, raised in the Temple, is called by the Lord who reaches down from a circular mandorla, like an open port-hole from heaven. Samuel hears only the call and answers to Eli, who bids him: 'Go and sleep. And if he shall call thee any more thou shalt say: Speak Lord, for thy servant heareth.' (2:9). Summoned again, Samuel is established as the leading prophet of Israel, 'And the word of Samuel came to pass to all Israel' (2:21).

And Samuel establishes the line of the Kings of Israel. Samuel (white bearded and haloed) meets Saul: 'And when Samuel saw Saul, the Lord said to him: Behold the man . . . This man shall reign over my people.' (9:17). The anointing of Saul as the first of the kings of Israel shows his stature: 'from his shoulders and upward he appeared above all the people' (9:2), as he crouches before Samuel, 'Behold, the Lord hath anointed thee to be the prince over his inheritance' (10:1).

The verso, which faced the historiated initial, tells of King David. Saul stands tall before his army as the boy David prepares to sling the fatal stone at Goliath. The huge figure of Goliath is described, 'And he had a helmet of brass upon his head; and he was clothed with a coat of mail with scales. And the weight of his coat of mail was five thousand sicles of brass. And he had greaves of brass on his legs; and a buckler of brass covered his shoulders.' (17:5–6). Goliath's height dominates the composition. He overlaps the frame and tops the central axis of the miniature formed by the tree and the column. The triumphant David severs the head with Goliath's own huge sword, as the Philistine horde retreats. David is able to soothe Saul's rage: 'So, whensoever the evil spirit from the Lord was upon Saul, David took his harp and played with his hand: and Saul was refreshed and was better, for the evil spirit departed from him.' (16:23). Yet Saul's jealousy bites repeatedly: 'And David played . . . And Saul held a spear in his hand, and threw it: and David stept aside . . . twice.' (18:10–11). David was destined to survive Saul's anger. Samuel had already anointed him king, as was told in 1 Kings 16, when, guided by God, he called the young shepherd boy from the fields: 'Now he was ruddy and beautiful to behold, and of a comely face. And the Lord said: Arise, and anoint him for this is he.' (16:12). This anointing was depicted symbolically in the initial to Genesis, but here it is a narrative, 'anointed among his brethren' (16:13), his father Jesse looking on. The narratives of the Morgan Leaf conclude with the death of Absalom, David's son. Like all fathers, David has overlooked his beloved son's treachery, and David's faithful servant Joab takes the chance offered when Absalom becomes caught by the hair in an oak tree. The sword of Joab is thrust through his body (2 Samuel (2 Kings) 18:9–18). Despite Absalom's crimes against his father, David mourns and, as David's servants tell of his death, 'the king covered his head, and cried with a loud voice: O my son Absalom, O Absalom my son, O my son!' (19:4).

The Morgan Leaf is the work of two artists. Both sides were designed by the Apocrypha Master, seen through pose and gesture, and his characteristic drawing style shows where fragments of paint have flaked off. The Apocrypha Master's designs are full of figures, overlapping and filling all the available space. In completing the painting, the Morgan Master reduced this crowding, even painting over the horses of Joab's companions to make space for his preferred solemn figures and horses.

While the distinction between the draughtsman and the painter is usually taken to be clear-cut, here both masters are involved in painting. The Apocrypha Master applied the gold and, on the recto, he set down the colours – the malachite green and bright orange, the pale fawn and the blue of the bed hangings. The rosette-like modelling of the folds of fabric between Samuel's feet and on Eli's orange bedding is his work also. Yet the painting of the faces and the completion of some of the drapery is without doubt the work of the Morgan Master, clearly seen in the strongly modelled face of the elderly Eli, and in Hannah's drapery as she bows before the altar. The distinct tonal impression from recto to verso, in particular the strongly coloured backgrounds on the verso, show that here the Morgan Master's own colour choices prevailed. The historiated initial 'F' is the work of the same two artists, the painting of the faces with the green modelling around the jaws and eyes all the work of the Morgan Master. The decorative motifs on the initial stem are his too, similar to the decorative initial to Ruth. Both decoratively and iconographically these three folios must have made a tremendous impact at the start of the Books of Kings.

2 Samuel (2 Kings), f.99v, figs. 4 and 36

The opening of the second book of Kings is grand in scale, although limited to the historiated initial. It is the first of a group of three initials designed by the Leaping Figures Master, although only the third, f.120v, was painted by him. The initial 'F', FACTUM EST AUTEM, 'Now it came to pass after the death of

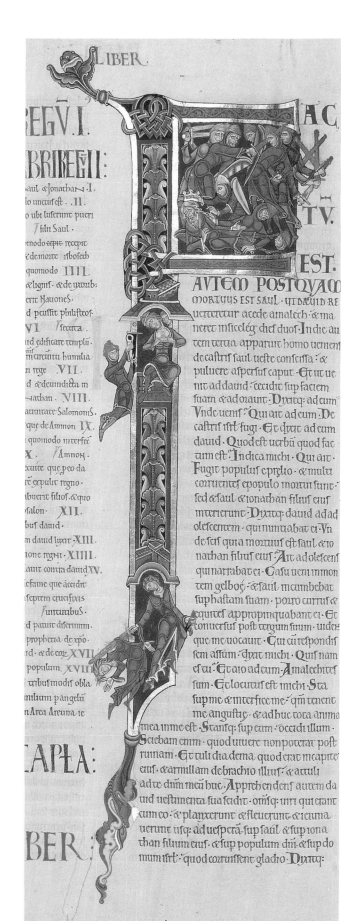

Saul', is 500mm. (19¾ins) in height, depicting the Battle of Mount Gelbo (1 Kings 31) where Saul lies dying with his sons. But the battle is described to David by the Amalekite in the opening of the second book, where he tells how he killed Saul at Saul's own request, and continues: 'And I took the diadem that was on his head, and the bracelet that was on his arm, and have brought them hither to thee, my lord. Then David took hold of his garments and rent them' (2 Kings (2 Samuel) 1:10–11). The anguished David is seated in a niche tearing his garment from his chest, as the Amalekite bends his knee to him in the space between the columns. David's rage later falls on the Amalekite, 'David said to him: Why didst thou not fear to put out thy hand to kill the Lord's anointed? And David calling one of his servants said: Go near and fall upon him. And he struck him so that he died.' (1:14–15). The lithe body of the Amalekite is bent in half by the weight of the sword blow.

Work on this initial was already well advanced by the Leaping Figures Master, with the old-style gold, the rich palette, the damp-fold form of the drapery, the poses and the physical angles of the figures already set out, and two of the faces complete, those of the murderer and the murdered Amalekite. The Amalekite Master, named for this initial, in fact only completed the detail of the drapery, smoothing the damp-fold, and modifying unfinished faces into pert profiles.

1 Kings (3 Kings), f.109, fig.37

The third Book of Kings opens in the last years of the life of David, ET REX D(AVID) SENUERAT 'Now King David was old'. David's promise to Bathsheba that her son Solomon would be king is fulfilled as David charges young Solomon, 'I am going the way of all flesh. Take thou courage, and shew thyself a man. And keep the charge of the Lord thy God, to walk in his ways, and observe his ceremonies, and his precepts and judgements and testimonies as it is written in the law of Moses . . .' (1 Kings (3 Kings) 2:2–3) David's servants were concerned for him: 'Let us seek for our lord the king a young virgin, and let her stand before the king, and cherish him, and sleep in his bosom and warm our lord the king . . . and they found Abishag a Shunammite . . . and the damsel was exceedingly beautiful . . .' (1:2–4). With the succession to the throne taken care of, David dies, comforted by Abishag.

In contrast to 2 Kings, where the Leaping Figures

36 (*Left*) 2 Samuel, the second book of Kings, f.99v, *Amalekite Master over a design of the Master of the Leaping Figures*

habebatq̄: g̃ranf plurimof dief · Cumq̄: opi
rcur uefbuf · non calefiebat · Dixerunt g̃
ferui fui · Quēramuf dño n̄ro regi · ad olefcen
tulam uirginem · & ftet coram rege & foueat
cum · dormiatq̄: infinu fuo · & calefaciat dñm

37 1 Kings, the third book of Kings, f.109, *Amalekite Master over a design of the Master of the Leaping Figures*

Master's mark is so firmly set, this initial shows more characteristics of the Amalekite Master. The figures have lost their vigour and move hesitantly, the drapery falling softly over their lax limbs, the pale palette distinctly different. Only the flat gold laid down by the designer constrained the Amalekite Master.

2 Kings (4 Kings), f.120v, figs. 2 and 38

This great initial shows the Leaping Figures Master's style at its most richly vigorous. The initial 'P', PREVARICATUS EST MOAB, 'And Moab rebelled against Israel', runs the full height of the page, creating three episodes. Ahaziah, king of Samaria, sent his messengers: 'Go, consult Beelzebub, the god of Ekron, whether I shall recover of this my illness' (2 Kings (4 Kings) 1:2). At the same time Elijah the prophet, was sent by God: 'Arise and go up and meet the messengers of the king of Samaria and say to them: Is there not a God in Israel that ye go to consult Beelzebub . . .?' (1:3). These messengers return to their king carrying the message he gave them: '. . . thus saith the Lord: From the bed on which thou art gone up, thou shalt not come down; but thou shalt surely die.' Ahaziah tries to appease Elijah and his God, and ultimately Elijah goes to him, but only to repeat the words: 'Because thou hast sent messengers to consult Beelzebub . . . thou shalt surely die.' (1:16).

The Leaping Figures Master uses the stem of the

38 2 Kings, the fourth book of Kings, f.120v, *Master of the Leaping Figures*

initial to whirl Elijah and his chariot to heaven. His companion Elisha asks: 'I beseech thee that in me may be thy double spirit, and he answered . . . if thou see me when I am taken from thee, thou shalt have what thou hast asked', and '. . . behold a fiery chariot, and fiery horses parted them both asunder: and Elijah went up by a whirlwind into heaven. And Elisha saw him and cried: My father, my father, the chariot of Israel and the driver thereof.' 'And he took up the mantle of Elijah, that fell from him' (2:9–12). The Leaping Figures Master shows the mantle twice, once golden with its sleeve raised to Elijah, and again, dark blue and shrunken, held up by Elisha, his head thrown back to watch the chariot, his cry 'My father, my father . . .' represented by his scroll.

The style and design is wholly characteristic of the Leaping Figures Master: the rich palette, the damp-fold drapery, the flame-like ground beneath the feet of Elijah, the heavy bunches of grapes, the tangled knot. It is among the greatest complete initials in the Bible, and the parchment, darkened by many years of lying open, demonstrates the importance of this opening.

Explicit/incipit

The end of the last complete quire of the Books of Kings became the end of Volume 1 when rebound in 1948.

Volume 2 (ff. 129–217)

Volume 2 opens on f. 129 with a new quire, the first two folios of which conclude the text of the Books of Kings. Volume 2 contains the prophetic books, from Isaiah to Malachi.

Isaiah, f. 131, figs. 16 and 39

Jerome's prologue to Isaiah on f. 130v, opens with a decorative painted initial, a serpent. Then, lacking its chapter headings, almost a whole empty column precedes the Book of Isaiah, with only the *incipit* at its base. The text begins: VISIO YSAIE, FILII AMOS, 'The vision of Isaias, the son of Amos'. The vision described is terrible: 'woe to the sinful nation, a people laden with iniquity, a wicked seed, ungracious children: they have forsaken the Lord.' (Isaiah 1:4) Here, the first initial in the Bible by the Gothic Majesty Master (also named the Isaiah Master), Isaiah calmly receives the prophecy in a scroll from God, betraying no hint of the terrors of the text. This static moment is characteristic of the somewhat bland compositions of this, probably the youngest of the artists to work on the Bible. This folio was added to the collation together with its cognate, f. 134, probably in substitu-

39 The Book of Isaiah, f. 131, *Gothic Majesty Master*

tion for a major text error, which could not be rectified through erasure. The scribe of these two leaves is the same as the main corrector of the 1170s, and is written to match the main hand as far as possible, although in a much blacker ink. Folio 134 has lost a small, probably decorative, initial (65 × 50mm., 2½ × 2ins). A remaining initial on this folio, unlike any other decorative initials in the Bible, is closely related to those in Winchester Cathedral MS 8, also from the cathedral scriptorium. This 'supply' bifolium provides a glimpse of the Bible manuscript in the latest stages of the work, with the corrector of the script throwing up his hands in horror at an error beyond repair, and re-writing it with its pair, to look as similar to the original as possible.

Jeremiah (Jeremias) f. 148, cover and fig. 40

Jerome's prologue to Jeremiah opens with a large painted initial 'I', followed by the *capitulae*, dividing the Book of Jeremiah into one hundred and thirty-four chapters. The historiated initial 'V' marks the start of the text, part way down the right hand column of the page. The contrast between the calling of Isaiah and that of Jeremiah could hardly be greater. Whereas Isaiah receives his vision of doom with composure, Jeremiah, in the hands of the Leaping Figures Master, reels back in horror at God's words to him. And, in contrast to the simple straight scroll handed from God to Isaiah, Jeremiah receives the word from God descending direct from heaven, his feet still among the

40 The Book of Jeremiah, f.148, *Master of the Leaping Figures*

21). The initial 'R' of the Prayer shows Jeremiah appealing to God. In contrast to the vigorous youth of f.148, the Jeremiah here is grey-bearded and overburdened with sorrow. His scroll of prayer rises from his hand to God above. The Morgan Master is at his most Byzantine in this initial, with God's blessing extended to the world like the Christ Pantocrator in the apse of Byzantine churches, most closely linked with the mosaics at Cefalu, Sicily, of *c.*1165. Byzantinism was not new in Winchester. Among the miniatures in the psalter of Bishop Henry is a pair of images copied from a Byzantine icon by an English artist. The contrast between this 'Byzantine' diptych and the main illumination is as great as that between the Jeremiahs of the Master of the Leaping Figures and the Morgan Master. Only a few folios apart, and painted with an interval of only few years between them, these two Jeremiahs demonstrate the change in English style from Romanesque to Byzantine-influenced 'transitional'.

Baruch f.169, figs. 22 and 42

On this same page, following the short prologue with its decorative initial 'L', the book of Baruch begins. Baruch, secretary and disciple of Jeremiah, follows his master's prophecy. While it begins with the destruction of Jerusalem, it goes on to rejoice: 'Put off, O Jerusalem, the garment of thy mourning and affliction: and put on the beauty and honour of that everlasting glory which thou hast from God' (Baruch 5:1). The written word, not direct inspiration from God, is the source of Baruch's prophecy: 'And Baruch read the words of this book in the hearing of Jechonias . . . and

clouds. 'And the Lord put forth his hand and touched my mouth. And the Lord said to me: Behold, I have given my words in thy mouth.' (Jeremiah 1:9) The words of the scroll, ECCE DEDI VERBA MEA I ORE TUO, are given in answer to Jeremiah's plaint 'A, a, a, Lord God, behold, I cannot speak, for I am a child' (1:6) as inscribed on his scroll, ECCE NESCIO LOQUI PUER EGO SUM. The drama of the calling of the prophet 'Before I formed thee in the bowels of thy mother, I knew thee: and before thou camest forth out of the womb I sanctified thee and made thee a prophet unto the nations' (1:5) is given full expression in the confrontation between these two figures, eyes fixed rigidly on each other, bodies twisting apart. God next tests his prophet: 'What seest thou, Jeremiah?' (1.11), and in the frame are the almond tree (1.11) lush in the background, and the face 'of the north' (1.13) in the finial.

Lamentations of Jeremiah f.157 – Prayer of Jeremiah f.169, figs. 22 and 41

The Lamentations of Jeremiah number the iniquities, the punishments and the bitterness of the people of Israel, and mourn the destruction of Jerusalem. Only a roughly cut hole remains in place of this initial. Chapter 5 of Lamentations is Jeremiah's prayer: 'Remember O Lord, what is come upon us: consider and behold our reproach.' (Lamentations 5:1), concluding 'But thou, O Lord, shalt remain for ever: thy throne from generation to generation . . . Convert us O Lord to thee, and we shall be converted . . .' (5:19–

41 The Prayer of Jeremiah, f.169, *Master of the Morgan Leaf*

42 The Book of Baruch, f.169, *Master of the Morgan Leaf*

in the hearing of all the people that came to hear the book.' (1:3). Jechonias listens, as do the attentive people within the city walls: 'in the hearing of the nobles the sons of the kings, and in the hearing of the ancients and in the hearing of the people, from the least even to the greatest of them that dwelt in Babylonia, by the river Sedi.' (1:4).

As is often found in this Bible, a pair of inscriptions is visible in the margin next to the initial. One provided the text for the rubricator, the other identified the scenes to be painted. However, the Morgan Master here did not comply with the instruction given but directly illustrated the opening words of the text.

Ezechiel, prologue f.170v, fig.43 and prophecy f.172, figs. 9 and 44

The prophecy of Ezechiel is preceded by a prologue with, unusually, an opening historiated initial. Jerome explains in his prologue how Ezechiel was captured with Joachim, king of Juda, and led into Babylon, here shown by the Morgan Master in a composition reminiscent of Christ taken by the Jews in Passion iconography. The captives of Babylon watch their arrival, behind the sealed gates of the city.

The book of Ezechiel opens with prophecy made apparent, '. . . when I was in the midst of the captives by the river Chobar, the heavens were opened and I saw the visions of God.' '. . . the likeness of four living creatures . . . the likeness of a man in them. Every one had four faces and every one had four wings. Their feet were straight feet and the sole of their foot was like the sole of a calf's foot: and they sparkled like the appearance of glowing brass.' '. . . there was the face of a man, and the face of a

lion . . . and the face of an ox . . . and the face of an eagle over all the four' (Ezechiel 1:5–10). 'Now as I beheld the living creatures, there appeared upon the earth by the living creatures one wheel with four faces . . . And the wheels had also a size and a height and a dreadful appearance: and the whole body was full of eyes round about all the four . . .' (1:15–18).

The design of the Morgan Master visually clarifies this obscure vision, a vision so difficult that, as St Jerome says in his letter to Paulinus, only the elders among the Hebrews were permitted to read it. The Morgan Master creates a tetramorph – a four-headed creature, the four faces of which became the symbolic four evangelists on whose words the New Testament relied. The wheels interlock, the four faces are lodged within their hubs, the multitude of eyes on the spokes. The creatures are winged: 'Every one with two wings covered its body, and the other was covered in like manner. And I heard the noise of their wings, like the noise of many waters, as it were the voice of the most high God.' (1:23–4). The tetramorph's wings are

43 Prologue to Ezechiel, f.170v, *Master of the Morgan Leaf*

44 The Book of Ezechiel, f.172, *Master of the Morgan Leaf*

depicted like those of the cherubim described in chapter 10, 'their whole body and their necks and their hands and their wings . . . were full of eyes' (10:12). While the meaning of these prophecies was much debated, the Morgan Master's half-literal interpretation, laid on the glittering surface of the initial, draws the essentials together – the inspired all-seeing evangelists, the interlocking of the wheels with the spirit: 'for the spirit of life was in the wheels' (1:20–1).

The Book of Daniel, ff.190, 193, figs. 45 and 46

Where the Morgan Master responds to the challenge of the visionary text of Ezechiel, he turns to a simple narrative for the book of the prophet Daniel, illustrating the capture of Jerusalem by King Nebuchadnezzar, king of Babylon, who favoured some of the captured children, 'a daily provision, of his own meat and of the wine of which he drank himself, that being nourished three years afterwards they might stand before the king'. (Daniel 1:5). The initial shows the child Daniel with two of his companions rejecting the golden cup: '(he) purposed in his heart that he would not be defiled with the king's table nor with the wine which he drank' (1:8). The master of the eunuchs, given charge of the children, understood, 'And God gave to Daniel grace and mercy in the sight of the prince of the eunuchs' (1:9), and the intensity of the revelation is shown on his face.

Chapter 5 of Daniel opens with the narrative of the great feast of King Belshazzar (Baltasar), BALTASAR REX FECIT GRANDE CONVIVIUM . . . when the fateful writing on the wall can be interpreted only by Daniel. But the scene is not illustrated. Instead, this initial is an inhabited tanglewood, characteristic of the work of the Apocrypha Master, which encloses a pair of figures confronted by bird-bodied beasts from whose mouths the decorative stem of the initial grows. This initial begins a sequence of designs by the Apocrypha Master, and yet the gilding and painting here was completed by the Morgan Master, the swirl of the drapery clearly his, the faces, despite their bright green flesh, solemn, on their bodies twisted by the Apocrypha Master's design.

The Minor Prophets, ff.197v–217

The books of the twelve minor prophets originally completed the first volume of the Winchester Bible, and now complete the second. It is a short section as each book is short, but each is illustrated, and some prologues also are illuminated, forming a rich section of illumination.

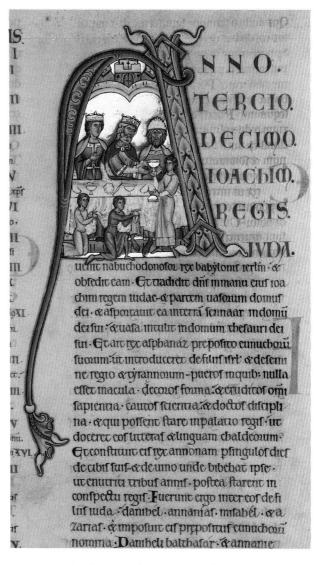

45 The Book of Daniel, f.190, *Master of the Morgan Leaf*

47 The Book of Hosea, f.198, *Master of the Apocrypha Drawings*

48 The Book of Joel, f.200v, *Master of the Apocrypha Drawings*

46 (*Left*) The Book of Daniel, f.193, *Master of the Morgan Leaf over a design of the Master of the Apocrypha Drawings*

Minor prophets, prologue, f.197v, fig.20 and Hosea (Osee), f.198, figs. 21 and 47

The opening on ff.197v–198 sets the style. A blue-bodied banner-carrying centaur, with battling beasts and men in a tanglewood, overfills the 'N' of the prologue to the minor prophets. The 'T' of the prologue to Hosea follows, which is concluded by a fine incipit, in uncial letters. And on the recto is the prophet Hosea preaching. The prophecy of the book of Hosea is an allegory of the fate of Israel, 'Hear ye the word of the Lord, ye children of Israel . . .' (Hosea 4:1). These two facing initials were both designed by the Apocrypha Master but, although the Hosea was completed by him, as shown by the use of flat gold and pale colours and his stylised use of line, the prologue initial was completed by the Morgan Master, who dotted the tanglewood with gessoed gold, while his evenly laid rich colour gives dignity to the clamberers.

Joel (Johel), f.200v, fig.48

The prologue initial, 'S', is cut out, and its hole cuts into the opening text of the book. Whereas Hosea addressed Israel, Joel addresses the old men of Judea: 'Hear this, ye old men . . .' (Joel 1:2). The words inscribed on his halo, the diapered gold on the blue initial ground, and the decorative rounded display letters, emphasised by a listener who points them out, are all decorative features found only in this one initial, yet characteristic of the Apocrypha Master – the elaborate linear drapery patterns, the prominent noses and heavy jaws, the huge drooping oval eyes, and the characteristic bright, pale colours. The words of Joel prophesy the coming of the Lord: 'And the Lord shall roar out of Sion and utter his voice from Jerusalem; and the Lord shall be the hope of his people and the strength of the children of Israel' (3:16); the Lord is shown as a haloed dove. Where the preaching of Hosea frightens off the Devil, Joel's preaching summons forth the sign of the Holy Spirit.

Amos, f.201v, fig.49

The prophet Amos was called upon to convey words of denunciation: 'The Lord will roar from Sion and . . . the shepherds shall mourn . . .' (Amos 1:2). He was a prophet 'among the herdsmen' and, in parallel with the image of the boy David in the psalter initial (see fig.59), he is shown wrestling a lion. To the design of the Master of the Leaping Figures, the Morgan Master completes the painting, laying gessoed gold, smoothing out the lines of the interlocking S-shaped figures. The simple formality of the key design

49 The Book of Amos, f.201v, *Master of the Morgan Leaf over a design of the Master of the Leaping Figures*

in the initial frame and the flow of the drapery show the changed nature of the design, one of the most satisfactory of the two-artist initials, despite the damaged state of the gold background.

Obadiah (Abdias), f.203v, figs. 24 and 50

The illustration reflects a belief that this Obadiah was also governor of the house of Achab, he who hid and sustained the persecuted prophets, 'For when Jezebel killed the prophets of the Lord, he took a hundred prophets and hid them . . . in caves, and fed them with bread and water' (3 Kings 18:4). The prison-like cave is sealed in darkness by the thickly gessoed gold. The Genesis Master's robust figures have almost overcome the sinuous quality of the Leaping Figures Master's design. The squared initial has a green edge around the gold frame and, in a layout unique within

50 The Book of Obadiah, f.203v, *Master of the Genesis Initial over a design of the Master of the Leaping Figures*

the Bible (although familiar in other, mostly later, examples), it encloses the gold display letters, set on coloured grounds. This initial was rediscovered by Oakeshott, who recognised the two artists' work. Yet this gothic-type display script suggests a different design of illumination. Had the cutting not fitted jigsaw-like into its space, its Winchester Bible origins would have been disputed. It stands as a reminder of the tremendous diversity found within the Bible.

Jonah, prologue, f.204, fig.51, prophecy, f.205v

This section of the manuscript has suffered more than its share of losses. The initial to the prologue of Jonah survives, illuminated and large in scale, the work of the Genesis Master, the S-form of the grinning dragon dominating the square, green-edged frame. It is the only purely decorative initial designed by the Genesis Master.

But the historiated initial to the text is cut out; at approximately 120×140mm. (4¾×5½ins), one of the largest losses. A fragment of green-edge may indicate another Genesis Master initial, and Jonah spat up on the shore of Nineveh by the whale is surely its subject.

Micah (Micheas), f.204v, figs. 8 and 52

This prophet, like Amos, wrestles with a lion. The prophecy of Micah is one of endless struggle, fighting iniquities, and promising: 'And thou Bethlehem Ephrata art a little one among the thousands of Juda: out of thee shall he come forth unto me that is to be the ruler in Israel . . .' (Micah 5:2). The Genesis Master works over the Leaping Figures Master design, and squares up the frame in a green edge, filling the corners with a patterned background. He had to leave a window for the FACTU already written in anticipation of the curve of the 'V'. The prophet grapples the lion's jaws apart, the solid youth transforming the Leaping Figures Master's graceful leap to one of determined concentration. The face of Micah, with the deep green shadows and undulating lines of the forehead setting off the intense dark eyes, shows this master at his Byzantine best.

Nahum, f.206v

Nahum foretells the destruction of the city of Nineveh. Preceded by two Jerome prologues, each with a decorative painted initial, the prophecy, in only three chapters, has lost its initial 'O', only leaving part of the square capitals display script.

51 The Prologue to Jonah, f.204, *Master of the Genesis Initial*

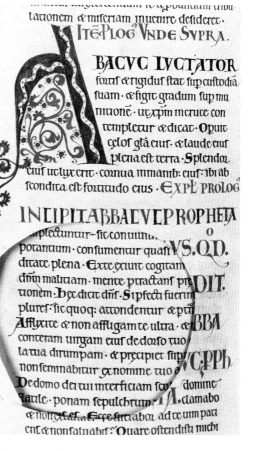

53 The Prologue and the Book of Habbakuk, initial cut out, f.207v

52 The Book of Micah, f.204v, *Master of the Genesis Initial over a design of the Master of the Leaping Figures*

Habakkuk (Habacuc) and the Prayer of Habakkuk, ff.207v–8, figs. 10 and 53

Habakkuk too is lost. Two painted initials to the prologues are followed by an 'O'-shaped hole, leaving the display letters to open the text. The initial to the prayer of Habakkuk is on the facing page, in shape a near match. Habakkuk's prayer is both prophecy and praise and concludes, 'The Lord God is my strength: and he will make my feet like the feet of harts. And he, the conqueror, will lead me upon my high places singing psalms.' (Habakkuk 3:19). Both the design and completion of this initial are the work of the Morgan Master, solemnity here giving way to grace. The gessoed gold stands proud of the parchment surface, and a black band surrounds the initial field, setting off the listening figure of Habakkuk: 'O Lord I have heard thy hearing' (3:2).

Zephaniah (Sophonias), f.210v, figs. 7 and 54

The image of Christ Pantocrator dominates this initial, as it does the Prayer of Jeremiah (f.169). Yet this Christ, borne up by angels, has an inflexible fierceness not shared by the Morgan Master's image. The text promises this visit, 'And it shall come to pass . . . that

54 The Book of Zephaniah, f.210v, *Master of the Genesis Initial over a design of the Master of the Apocrypha Drawings*

I will visit in that day upon every one that entereth arrogantly . . . that fill the house of the Lord their God with iniquity and deceit.' (Zephaniah 1:8–9). The Apocrypha Master's design has been smothered by the Genesis Master's handling of the drapery and faces, his strong palette overcoming the decorative line, although the saffron yellow and malachite green of the elders flanking the front suggest that the Apocrypha Master had blocked in colour, as well as laying the flat gold.

Haggai (Aggeus), prologues and text. ff.209v,210, figs. 55 and 56

Overleaf Jerome's prologue to Haggai and Zechariah opens with an illuminated 'S', full of the entangled foliage of the Apocrypha Master, yet with the gessoed gilding and the intense and furrowed faces – brilliant in red and blue – of the Genesis Master. And four athletic nudes, blue and red, leap from the tangled core of the initial, their bodies boldly modelled in white.

Both this and the next prologue initial, to Haggai alone, show the Genesis Master simplifying and giving space to the foliage design. The gold of the upper part of the initial to Haggai was laid by the designer, but below the central medallion it is gessoed. The three narrative medallions show the prophet Haggai, dressed as a Crusader, conveying God's command to Zorobabel the king, telling him to restore the temple of Jerusalem, 'And the word of the Lord came by the hand of Haggai the prophet, saying: Is it time for you to dwell in ceiled houses, and this house lie desolate?'

55 The Prologue and the Book of Haggai, f.210, *Master of the Genesis Initial over a design of the Master of the Apocrypha Drawings*

56 The Prologue to Haggai and Zechariah, f.209v, *Master of the Genesis Initial over a design of the Master of the Apocrypha Drawings*

58 The Book of Malachi, f.213v, *Master of the Genesis Initial*

(Haggai 1:3–4). This prophecy was equally current in its demand in the twelfth century, recalling the Crusades to restore Jerusalem's holy places to Christianity; the Christianity that is prophesied by Haggai.

Zechariah (Zacharias), prologue and text f.210v, fig.57

The Apocrypha Master's design is all-but obliterated by the overpainting of the Genesis Master in these two initials, the prologue, with the fierce face glaring from the funnel-shaped horizontal of the 'Z', and the initial to the prophetic text, with the neat four medallions of the 'I' which illustrate the whole prophecy. Zechariah is reassured by an angel who pledges to explain his revelations (1:9) which are then depicted: the four smiths (1:20), the man with the measuring line, 'And I said: Whither goest thou? And he said to me: to

57 The Prologue and the Book of Zechariah, f.210v, *Master of the Genesis Initial over a design of the Master of the Apocrypha Drawings*

measure Jerusalem . . .' (2:1–2); and at the base, the clothing of Joshua the High Priest with clean clothes, 'And they put a clean mitre upon his head and clothed him with garments' (3:5).

Malachi (Malachias), f.213v, fig.58

The final prophecy, of Malachi, is brief: 'The burden of the word of the Lord to Israel, by the hand of Malachi' (1:1). God within the mandorla, here designed and painted by the Genesis Master, commands Malachi with a gesture, passing down the word as a scroll. 'Wherein hast thou loved us?' (1:2), asks Malachi, twisting to turn upwards to the Lord. Unaccountably the second column of this text was not completed by the main scribe, leaving the corrector scribe – the scribe of the bifolium in Isaiah – the task of completing the text, the final text of the original Volume 1.

Volume 3 (ff.218–330)

Psalms, ff.218–258

The Psalms of David opened the original second volume of the Winchester Bible. The opening leaf has been cut out (the first folio of the first quire), carrying with it the quire number, which shows that this leaf was in place when the Bible was first bound. It is possible, even likely, that this leaf was illuminated, a grand opening to the original Volume 2, in keeping with the opening to the books of Kings. The psalter is divided into four major sections, following the traditional Anglo-Saxon divisions.

Psalm 1, f.218, figs. 6 and 59

This volume now opens directly with the text of Psalm 1, the two columns now used to set in parallel the two versions of the psalms, the Gallican, the translation by St Jerome which found greatest acceptance in the western church, and the Hebraeorum, also a translation made by St Jerome, but this time going back, beyond the old Roman versions and beyond the Greek to the original Hebrew text. Each version opens with a large-scale historiated initial 'B', but without the opening words of the psalm BEATUS VIR, 'Blessed is the man', which was to have been painted in display script.

These two initials are typologically illustrated, with scenes from the life of David, composer of the psalms, set next to scenes of Christ. The young David, justifying his wish to tackle Goliath, had told Saul of his battles to protect his sheep: 'For I thy servant have killed both a lion and a bear: and this uncircumcised Philistine shall be also as one of them' (1 Kings 17:36). Symbolically, as was the case for the illustration to the book of the prophet Micah, these scenes are of the triumph of good over evil. The two scenes opening the Hebraeorum bear a parallel message, although from the New Law not the Old. Just as David releases the sheep from the jaws of the lion, so Christ releases the boy possessed of the Devil, 'And Jesus rebuked the unclean spirit and cured the boy and restored him to his father . . . but while all wondered at the things he did, he said to his disciples: Lay you up in your hearts these words, for it shall come to pass that the Son of Man shall be delivered into the hands of men.' (St Luke 9:43–4). The parallel to this scene is the Harrowing of Hell, Christ releasing the souls from the mouth of the Devil – an essential tenet of Christian faith, expressed in the *Credo*, a part of every celebration of Mass: '. . . crucified, died and was buried: He descended into Hell . . .'. The Harrowing of Hell demonstrates the power of Christ to save souls. Two contemporary examples of this scene survive at Winchester, in the psalter of Henry of Blois (f.24) and in the wall painting scheme in the Holy Sepulchre Chapel of the cathedral.

The Master of the Leaping Figures designed these two initials and completed laying on the gold, including the gilded fluttering hems. But the Genesis Master painted the design, softening the drapery and imparting fierceness to the faces through their heavy-browed eyes and strong jaws.

Psalm 51, f.232, figs. 19 and 60

The second section of the psalter begins with Psalm 51. The pair of illuminated 'Q's has no display lettering, QUID GLORIAS. The two scenes of the story, told in the two initials, are from the first book of Kings, (1 Samuel (1 Kings) 22). David, distrusted and harried by Saul, is urged to flee. Saul's servant Doeg reveals that he had been seen with Ahimelech the priest and with other priests. Saul is obsessed by his belief in David's disloyalty and orders all the priests to be killed, but it is only Doeg, armed with the sword of Goliath, who will do so. 'And the king said to Doeg: Turn thou and fall upon the priests. And Doeg the Edomite turned, and fell upon the priests, and slew in that day eighty-five men . . .' (22:18). The death of St Thomas Becket in 1170, murdered at the order of the king, in the presence of his priests at Canterbury, was an event which shocked the whole country – even the bishops. These initials may have been completed before that date, and therefore not inspired by this murder, but the impact of their gilded brutality would have been starkly resonant in 1170.

59 Psalm 1, f.218, *Master of the Genesis Initial over a design of the Master of the Leaping Figures*

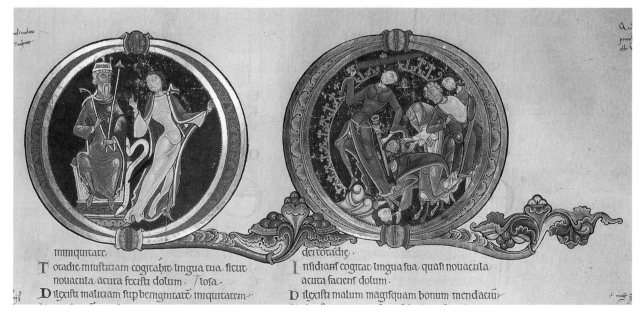

60 Psalm 51, f.232, *Master of the Leaping Figures*

61. Psalm 101, f.246, *unfinished, Master of the Morgan Leaf over a design of the Master of the Leaping Figures*

The Master of the Leaping Figures both designed and painted these initials, their gilded frames with lush foliage terminals reminiscent of a pair of enamelled belt buckles. The eagerness of the murderous Doeg is belied by the delicacy and elegance of his form – beheading the priests becomes ballet in this artist's style. The precision of the execution of the decorative work – the tiny white dots which surround the blue ground of the command of Saul, the gilded fretwork of the murder scene – characterise this master's work.

Psalm 101, f.246, figs. 15 and 61

The initials of Psalm 101 were left unfinished, but only after the painting was under way. The two initials show God's punishment of David for numbering the people of Israel (2 Samuel (2 Kings) 24) with three days of pestilence. Then, 'the Lord had pity on their affliction and said to the angel that slew the people: It is enough. Now, hold thy hand.' (24:16). David, as commanded, set up an altar on the threshing floor of Aruena, 'And David built there an altar to the Lord, and offered holocausts and peace-offerings'. God's covenant with Abraham is maintained, as is recalled in the text of Psalm 104: 'He is the Lord our God: his

judgements are in all the earth. He hath remembered his covenant for ever which he commanded to a thousand generations.' (Ps.104:7–8).

The Leaping Figures Master designed, gilded and painted the initial frames. The Morgan Master's unfinished overpainting has softened the damp-fold drapery into smooth heavy hangings, the complex folds of the blue robe of God comparable with the drapery on the verso of the Morgan Leaf. Most faces show the green tones of the underpainting, but the richly finished faces of the kneeling Abraham and the Angel of Death in the left initial show the completed form towards which the Morgan Master was progressing, modifying his fellow-artist's design as he went.

Psalm 109, f.250, fig.62

This psalm, DIXIT DOMINUS, 'The Lord said to my Lord: sit thou at my right hand' (Ps.109:1), celebrates the Trinity, anticipating Christ. The initial to the Gallican version of the psalm, on the left, illustrates the opening words, not completed by the rubricator, with the two identical persons of God enthroned like twins, their right hands raised in blessing, open books in their left hands. The Dove of the Holy Spirit hangs between them. All three wear identical haloes, with three gilded spokes, usually interpreted as 'cruciform', symbolic of Christ, but evidently used here (and elsewhere in the Bible) to indicate God in the Trinity.

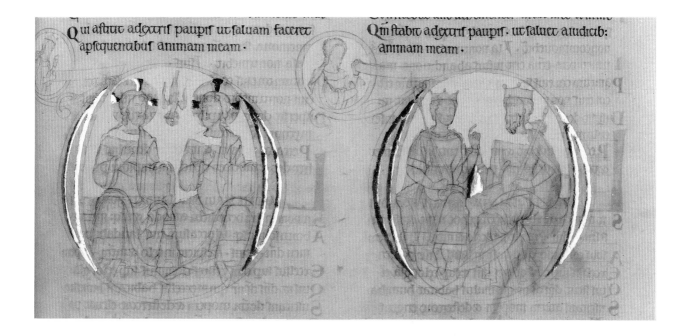

Qui afturc adextrif paupif ut saluam faceret apsequentrabus animam meam ·

Qm stabit adextrif paupif · ut saluet audicab: animam meam ·

62 Psalm 109, f.250, *unfinished, Gothic Majesty Master*

The crowned kings in the second initial bear sceptres, and the elder figure holds the wrist of the younger whose raised hand instructs, 'The Lord will send forth the sceptre of thy power out of Sion: rule thou in the midst of thy enemies.' (109:2). Above both initials are scroll-bearing figures, fingers raised in prophecy, 'With thee is the principality in the day of thy strength, in the brightness of thy saints: from the womb before the daystar I begot thee' (109:3).

This is the first design in the Bible left totally uncoloured. But it is gilded on the initial frame, with gesso laid in readiness for gold on the whole background surface. The Master of the Gothic Majesty was named by Oakeshott for these initials, and the balanced pose of the figures, the security of form, the soft style of the drawing all connect them to the Isaiah initial (f.131). His work exudes neither drama nor solemnity, having a simple and bland seriousness, soft and subtle in expression. Oakeshott recognised that, despite the softness of this style – more 'gothic' in spirit than any other work in the Bible – it is contemporary with the later work in the Bible.

The Books of Solomon, *ff.259–278*

The Books of Solomon, Proverbs (Parables), Ecclesiastes, Song of Songs and Wisdom, followed by Ecclesiasticus, form the next section in the Bible. The sequence is preceded by a prologue of St Jerome relating to the first three books of Solomon, which is marked by a large painted initial.

Proverbs (Parables), f.260, figs. 26 and 63

Solomon, the son of David, sets out his wisdom in the form of parables, '. . . to give subtlety to little ones, to the young man knowledge and understanding. A wise man shall hear and shall be wiser: and he that understandeth shall possess governments.' (Proverbs 1:4–5). Typical of the Leaping Figures Master the message is passed via a long and curling scroll – unlettered here. The elder responds to the gesture of Solomon, passing the message back to the young man.

This initial, like those for Psalms 101 and 109, provides a glimpse of the artist at work. The gold background and gold bars to the vertical stem of the 'P', are similar to the intentions of the Gothic Majesty Master in Psalm 109, but the figures and the layout of the composition were the work of the Leaping Figures Master. Probably further figures were obliterated by the gessoed gold. The painting at first glance looks complete, yet the faces and hair of all three figures, and the drapery of the young man remain at only the first stage of underpaint. The delicate facial modelling creating these bland expressions confirms that the Gothic Majesty Master contributed to the completion of this initial also. This forms his final contribution to the Bible, with three of the four initials in which his hand may be discerned left incomplete.

Ecclesiastes, f.268, fig.64

'Vanity of vanities, said Ecclesiastes: vanity of vanities and all is vanity.' (Ecclesiastes 1:2). The book of Ecclesiastes the preacher sets out a catalogue of the futilities of earthly desires and pleasures, 'what is it that hath been? The same thing that shall be. What is

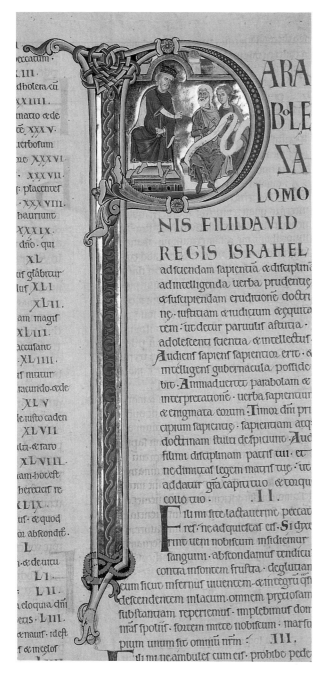

63 The Book of Proverbs, f.260, *unfinished, Gothic Majesty Master over a design of the Master of the Leaping Figures*

the structure of the damp-fold drapery, with thin parallel lines like contours on a map. In contrast to the Gothic Majesty Master's drawing for Psalm 109, there is no soft modelling with the pencil and the lines are partly over-drawn with pen as a preliminary to painting. These pen lines guide the painted contours, applied over the first layers of colour, forming the characteristic damp-fold drapery.

Song of Songs, f.270v, figs. 18 and 65

The initial to the Song of Songs demonstrates this perfectly, particularly in the robe of the Queen of Sheba, and here this master's links with the artists of the Bury Bible and the Lambeth Bible are at their most telling. The Song of Songs is a love poem, fitting to

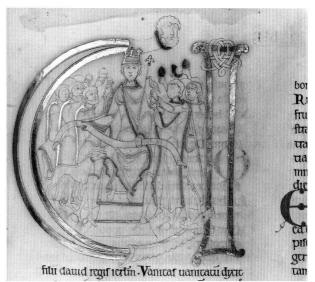

64 Ecclesiastes, f.268, *unfinished, Master of the Leaping Figures*

65 The Song of Songs, f.270v, *Master of the Leaping Figures*

it that hath been done? The same that shall be done.' (1:9). Seated on his throne, surrounded by his courtiers each bearing a temptation, the stony-faced king ignores them all. The falcon, the golden drinking horn, the hunting dogs, the rings and mirrors, all are rejected, as the king holds firmly onto this text, on a long scroll.

The gilding is complete on the initial frame, the crown and the hems of the cloaks, but otherwise this initial is no more than a drawing, revealing the Leaping Figures Master's sinuous style, and demonstrating the temperament of Solomon, as is revealed in the extravagant descriptions of his house and his temple, and the house of his wife, the Queen of Sheba (1 Kings (3 Kings) 10:5–7), and her exotic gifts to him: 'Thy wisdom and thy works exceed the fame which I heard . . . and she gave the king a hundred and twenty talents of gold and of spices a very great store and precious stones' (10:7,10). The text opens: 'Let him kiss me with the kiss of his mouth: for thy breasts are better than wine, smelling sweet of the best ointments. Thy name is as oil poured out: therefore young maidens have loved thee', 'I am black but beautiful O ye daughters of Jerusalem, as the tents of Cedar, as the curtains of Solomon' (Song of Songs 1:1–2 and 4). Yet this outpouring of human emotion, full of similes worthy of the metaphysical poets, has from the earliest of times been 'deconstructed' to form an allegory of Christ and his Church. This allegory is often reflected in the imagery accompanying the Song of Songs. This may take a variety of forms, but frequently Ecclesia, the woman symbolic of the Christian Church, is seated in the company of Christ, and sometimes they kiss. Here, however, the narrative is adhered to, and the artist shows King Solomon in company with his Queen, the Queen of Sheba, crowned and richly robed and seated within a house of many domes and towers.

Wisdom, f.272v, figs. 1 and 66

The Book of Wisdom, LIBER SAPIENTIE SALOMONIS, is Solomon's book of exhortations, urging the exercise of good government and justice. While these are the sentiments of Solomon, the authorship is less certain, and the illustration suggests that it is the work of the Wise Man, seated to the left, who, in presenting his book to Solomon and his fellow rulers, points out its precepts with determination. Solomon accepts and agrees. In this initial, fully completed by the Master of the Leaping Figures, the solemnity almost equals that of the Morgan Master, although created through the linear definition of the faces and eyes, not modelling. An elaborate townscape frames the image, the towers and roofs of twelfth-century England transformed into Solomon's kingdom.

Ecclesiasticus, f.278v, figs. 23 and 67

The last book of this section is not part of Solomon's books, although usually it is set at the end of them, as here. It is the book written by Jesus, son of Syrach of Jerusalem, and accepted into the Christian canon from earliest times. The text is again exhortation, defining the virtues, which were to become doctrine. The first chapter speaks of Wisdom, 'The word of God on high is the fountain of wisdom: and her ways are everlasting

66 The Book of Wisdom, f.272v, *Master of the Leaping Figures*

67 Ecclesiasticus, f.278v, *unfinished, Master of the Leaping Figures*

commandments.' (Ecclesiasticus 1:5). Enthroned, Wisdom here symbolises other virtues also. Her sceptre is the sceptre of faith, 'for the fear of the Lord is wisdom . . . and that which is agreeable to him is faith . . .' (1:34–5). Her pose, her book of Wisdom held up, is that of justice, 'Son, if thou desire wisdom, keep justice and God will give her to you' (1:33).

Just like the initial to Ecclesiastes, this is the raw design of the Master of the Leaping Figures, with only the gilded edges picked out. However, the coloured display script – the first occurrence in this volume of complete opening words to the text – creates the impression of this initial being more complete.

*Chronicles I and II (Paralipomenon I and II), f.293
and f.303, figs. 68 and 69*

There is only one single further historiation in this, the
first half of the second volume. Chronicles is frequently found immediately following the Books of
Kings, to which it forms a supplement – containing
'the things omitted'. In this version, as in the Bodleian
Winchester Bible, Chronicles follows Ecclesiasticus.
The first book starts on f.293, following its prologue,
the chapter headings, and a full rubric. However, the
opening initial to the text, 'A', is not even marked out;
it remains as it did when the scribe simply left the
necessary A-shaped space.

For the second book, f.303, the initial is designed
and gilded. It is again the work of the Leaping Figures
Master. The text tells of Solomon going to the 'high
place of Gabaon, where was the tabernacle of the
covenant of the Lord' (2 Chronicles 1:3). The moment
illustrated is described in verse 7: 'And behold, that
night God appeared to him saying: Ask what thou wilt

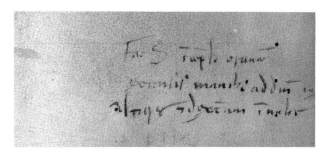

69 The second book of Chronicles, f.303, marginal
instruction to the illuminator

that I should give thee'. Solomon reaches forward in
response to the hand of God, extended from a glory
above the tabernacle lamps which hang over the ark
of the covenant. In the margin of this initial, like many
others, a trace of the instruction to the illuminator can
be seen, which here remains partially legible – 'Fac
S(olomon) i templo . . . manibus ad dm'. Here, unlike
the book of Baruch where the initial was designed and
painted by the Morgan Master, the Leaping Figures
Master followed the instruction given. The clarity of
the drawn and gilded design has been spoilt by the
application of some colour to the face and the upper
part of the body – not by the hand of the master. Yet
the articulation of the damp-fold drapery is at its most
rich, particularly on the extended leg of Solomon. The
display script is incomplete, and the initial sits in a
large space, lacking the incipit above and the opening
of the text below.

Job, f.316v, Tobias, f.326v, Preface to Judith, f.329v

At the end of this volume, these final 13 folios, are full
of plans, but empty even of designs. The prologues to
these books have completed painted decorative initials,
each large scale and elaborate, as shown in the extravagant 'A' for the prologue to Judith. The book of Job
starts with only an empty initial space. A folio has
been cut out here, which would have faced the preface
to Job on f.316, and which was possibly (or intended
to be) a full historiated page.

The preface to the book of Tobias opens facing a full
blank verso, and the outline form of the 'T' is only
sketched in, the text for the rubricator supplied in the
margin, 'Tobias ex tribu' The instruction to the illuminator is in the margin also, but it passes up the
responsibility for determining the subject, saying simply, 'Ad placitum', 'as you like'. The blank folio
facing Tobias, and the cut out leaf facing Job may both
have been intended to be full miniatures. The miniature facing the book of Judith is set on the verso of an
inserted folio which, in the original volume 2,
immediately followed this section.

68 The second book of Chronicles, f.303, *unfinished, Master
of the Leaping Figures*

Volume 4 (ff.331v–486): Judith to Apocalypse

Judith, f.331v, fig.14

The book of Judith contains, like the books of Job and Tobias, and of Esther, a story of the exploits of a single figure – Job, tormented by God but never failing in his patient acceptance of his lot; Tobias, blinded by God to test his faith and that of his son; and Judith, her courage pitted against Holofernes. He, the general of the armies of Nebuchadnezzar, had been sent, 'Go out against all the kingdoms of the west, and against them especially that despised my commandment. Thy eye shall not spare any kingdom: and all the strong cities thou shalt bring under my yoke.' (Judith, 2:5–6). Holofernes' success was total: 'all that resisted him he slew with the edge of his sword' (2:16). Only Jerusalem held out, and Achior spoke for the Israelites to Holofernes, fuelling his rage. The three registers of drawing on the folio facing the start of the book of Judith take up the story here, with Holofernes commanding Achior to be delivered up to the Israelites. His men, in fear, bind him to a tree. But Judith, a virtuous widow, resolved to defeat Holofernes by deceit. She prayed, and then she dressed up: 'she took off her haircloth and put away the garments of her widowhood. And she washed and anointed herself with the best ointment, . . . and the Lord also gave her more beauty because all this dressing-up did not proceed from sensuality but from virtue' (10:2–4). She gains admission to Holofernes' feast, and flatters both him and his cause. He falls into her power 'And Holofernes was made merry on her occasion, and drank exceeding much wine.' (12:20). The rest was easy, although her courage needed the support of her prayers. With the head of Holofernes in her hand she is able to pass on that courage to the people: 'hang ye up this head upon our walls. And as soon as the sun shall rise, let every man take his arms: and rush ye out . . . as making an assault' (14:1–2). Holofernes' chamberlain, discovering the body, cried out, 'One Hebrew woman hath made confusion in the house of King Nebuchadnezzar. For behold, Holofernes lieth upon the ground and his head is not upon him' (14:16). The army of Holofernes is defeated, and in the midst of the battle, haloed by an Israelite shield, Judith stands triumphant.

The book of Judith is full of visual detail and drama, excellent material for illustration. Yet the Apocrypha Master's outline drawing is incomplete, with many details still to be added. Although the frame is indicated and the intervals between the three registers are clear, no decoration is begun. Simply outlined as they

are, the sinuous, light-footed elegance of these figures, with their characteristic poses and drapery – the flying cloak, the canopied bed, the feast like that of Elkanah on f.88 – defines the style of this artist. The space for the text initial on the facing folio should surely have been his to complete.

Esther, f.337

Esther also begins with only a space, a vertical column for the 'I', IN DIES ASSUERUS measures approximately 350mm. × 80mm. Instructions for the illuminator were written in two registers, providing information for three separate scenes. At the top, 'Fac regem sedentem in sedie . . .', (Make the king sitting on a seat . . .), with the second stage to depict the king with the queen, and the lowest scene, 'fac unum suspensum . . .' (make a man hanged). The subjects of the initial are defined, although the illuminator would still have needed help from the text to set out the detail. And the instructions leave the artist free to determine the style, decoration and palette. Had this been completed by the Apocrypha Master (the artist of most of this section) he would surely have filled up the spaces between the historiated medallions with a tanglewood, as he did in completing the next initial, to Ezra.

Ezra, f.342, fig.70 and back cover

The Book of Ezra opens with a full height painted initial, the last completed initial in the Bible. At 400mm. (15¾ins) it is even taller than the Esther initial. In the midst of a tanglewood, full of characteristic creatures, narrative scenes are enclosed in a complex architectural tower. The text opens with the proclamation of King Cyrus, 'The Lord the God of heaven hath given to me all the kingdoms of the earth, and he hath charged me to build him a house (a temple) in Jerusalem . . .' (Ezra 1:2). This proclamation was given 'in writing also' (1:1) and, as the black painted scroll lies across the knees of Cyrus, its message is distributed by his messengers. But the building of the temple is thwarted, the proclamation disputed, and ultimately Ezra, both scribe and priest, takes to himself the task of bringing the law to the children of Israel, scattered by the captivity, '. . . they spoke to Ezra the scribe to bring the book of the law . . . which the Lord had commanded to Moses . . . he stood upon a step of wood . . . and Ezra opened the book before all the people: for he was above all the people . . . and Ezra blessed the Lord the great God. And all the people answered: Amen, Amen; lifting up their hands' (2 Ezra 8:1–6). The Apocrypha Master fills in the detail, including the many tabernacles, 'And they

made themselves tabernacles every man on the top of his house . . . and in the street of the water gate . . . and all the assembly of them . . . made tabernacles and dwelt in tabernacles.' (8:16–7). The familiar palette of the Apocrypha Master, these greens, pale blues, pinks and yellows, (the dominant colours of the recto of the Morgan Leaf) shine out, here untouched by another artist.

Maccabees, f.350v, fig.71

The second full-page drawing, again the work of the Apocrypha Master, faces the opening of the Book of Maccabees. This folio is part of the structure of the quire, but has not been ruled for text, evidently already designated for painting. Like the Judith page, even the drawing is unfinished, with no decorative border yet supplied. The book of Maccabees tells of King Antiochus who set up idols and outlawed the Jewish rites. The narrative of the miniature begins as his proclamation is delivered by the king to his soldiers (1 Maccabees 1:46–54). Mathathias the priest resists. He kills the Jew who agreed to sacrifice to the idol, shown still on its perch. And he kills the servant of Anthiocus who forced the Jew to break his faith (2:23–5). He appointed his son Judas Maccabeus to continue the struggle, whose way was always armed resistance, and 'they fought with cheerfulness the battle of Israel' (3:2). The enemies' leader, Nicanor, came with a great army but attempted to deceive Judas Maccabeus with peaceable words: 'Let there be no fighting between me and you.' But 'the enemies were prepared to take away Judas by force'. (7:28–9). And, as is shown, 'The armies joined battle . . . Nicanor was defeated, and slain . . . and they cut off Nicanor's head and his right hand which he had proudly stretched out, and hung it up over against Jerusalem.' (7:43–47). At the next battle the luck of Judas Maccabeus runs out and he is slain: 'How is the mighty man fallen that saved the people of Israel.' (9:21). He was buried in the family sepulchre, 'And all the people of Israel bewailed him with great lamentation . . .' (9:20), the cloak of one of the mourners rising into a flourished finial as he lays the shrouded form into the elaborate sepulchre.

The Apocrypha Master demonstrates in each of his four miniature pages that he is, above all, a narrative artist, using the space to tell the story with clarity and colour. Comparing the thickly populated miniature of Maccabees with the verso of the Morgan Leaf confirms that the number of figures and horsemen

70 The Book of Ezra, f.342, *Master of the Apocrypha Drawings*

71 The Book of Maccabees, f.350v, *unfinished, Master of the Apocrypha Drawings*

have there been reduced. The armies of Judas Macca-beus and his enemy are multitudinous and overlap-ping, a challenge which suits the Apocrypha Master who is at his most certain when filling a space with layers of crowded figures. Had the Morgan Master overpainted the Maccabees composition he would surely have reduced the hordes and simplified the setting.

The text initial is left with a space and a brief instruction, part of which again provides artistic free-dom, 'ad placitum'. There are no further designs by this master in the manuscript. And no further initials are painted. From this point on, the work is entirely undertaken by the Master of the Leaping Figures, and nothing is completed beyond the drawing and gilding stage.

2 Maccabees, f.363

The initial to the second part of Maccabees is designed, following instructions still legible in the margin, to show the sacrifice of Nehemiah (2 Maccabees 1:20–22), and the kindling of fire, as water was poured over the great stones of the altar (2 Maccabees 1:31–2). The drawing is complete, with careful delineation of the drapery, by the Leaping Figures Master, and the gold has been applied, directly onto the parchment as was his procedure, around the edge of the initial and the hems of the garments.

With the conclusion of the book of Maccabees, on f.374v, the Old Testament is complete.

New Testament, ff.371–486

This section of the Bible would undoubtedly have been the richest section of all. It exceeds even the Minor Prophets section in the multitude of major openings and the rich use of painted decorative initials. The 17 drawn designs, some historiated, some decora-tive, are all the work of the Leaping Figures Master. Often, in the margin next to one of these initials, or next to a space, there is an instruction defining the subject for the illuminator, and these instructions always open with 'Fac': make, or do. This section provides evidence of the Leaping Figures Master in total control as the designer, and the complexity of these page layouts, with the complex apparatus of prefaces, prologues and expositions (entitled 'argumen-tum') suggest the close cooperation between designer and scribe. Whereas other parts of the Bible show the artist responsible overlapping the text, or not filling the space available, the intimate infilling of initial spaces is everywhere evident in this New Testament section. Where earlier in the Bible the omission of

display script is common, suggesting that this would be a final procedure once the initial was completed and in place, here the display lettering is always complete – incipit, explicit and the opening words of the texts.

At this point, following the opening texts of the Eusebian concordance, three folios have been removed – cut from the collation. The lost pages might have contained full miniatures, narratives of the Gospel stories following the form of the Judith and Maccabees pages. More likely, however, they contained the canon tables, the tables of textual comparison which provide the essential cross-references and indexes to the gospel stories. Canon tables were frequently richly decorated, and would usually include the evangelist symbols. The designs that the Leaping Figures Master might have made, with decorative columns on six pages of tables, may still survive.

Prologue of St Jerome, f.375

The prologue to the four gospels written by St Jerome was among his very first works, accompanying the translations of the gospels made at the request of Pope Damasus in c.382, while still in Rome. Reflecting this, the Jerome seated at the top of this initial is young and lithe, a very different figure from those painted by the Genesis Master on ff.1 and 3. Apart from those first two, no other prologue in the Bible is illustrated. The importance of this initial reflects the huge importance of the next sequence of texts, the four Gospels of the New Testament. The prologue describes the circum-stances in which the new gospel translations were made and, through references back to former writers and translators, confirms their authority, and their truth.

In this initial, the whole array of display script is complete, and the artist has supplied the complete design, the young haloed figure poised elegantly at his writing desk in the top of the 'P', PLURES FUISSE.

The St Jerome preface is followed by a number of further prefaces and the argumentum, before the first Gospel text of St Matthew opens on f.376v.

St Matthew, f.376v

Surprisingly, this first gospel opens with only a decorative initial. Elaborate though this is, a design by the Leaping Figures Master at his richest and most complex, it contributes to the supposition that some historiation has been lost in this section. It is not gilded, although it has a full and complete set of display capitals to start the text.

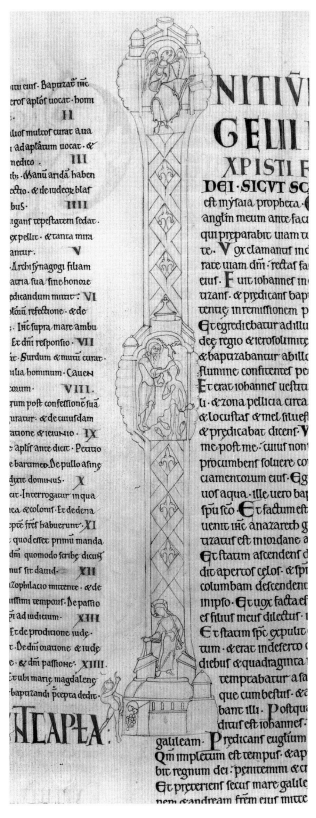

72 The Gospel of St Mark, f.387v, *unfinished, Master of the Leaping Figures*

St Mark, f.387v, fig.72

The initial to St Mark demonstrates how closely knit is the initial design with the space left available. The artist has designed a three-tier initial 'I', with the space for historiation fitted into the architectural structure. The decoration of the stem with the three-dimensional lattice enclosing a fleur-de-lys is not seen elsewhere in this manuscript. The evangelist is writing his gospel, laid on a lectern. He is nimbed, and his head is in the form of a lion; his symbol, drawn from the prophecy of Ezechiel (see p.43). The lower two medallions relate closely to the Gospel text – so closely that the illustration occurs directly next to the writing of the episode. Christ is baptised – John the Baptist, preaching and baptising in the river Jordan, foretold the coming of Christ: 'There cometh after me one mightier than I, the latchet of whose shoes I am not worthy to stoop down and loose' (Mark 1:7). Jesus came to be baptized and: 'he saw the heavens opened and the Spirit as a Dove descending' (Mark 1:10). No dove is portrayed here, but the hand of God from the opened glory of heaven illustrates the next verse, 'And there came a voice from heaven: Thou art my beloved Son: in thee I am well pleased.' (Mark 1:11). The account of the temptation is simply stated by St Mark: 'and (he) was tempted by the Devil' (1:13). The account in St Matthew tells of the three temptations of the Devil before Christ sends him away. The illustration here depends on that version: 'Begone Satan! For it is written, The lord thy God shalt thou adore and him only shalt thou serve.' (Matthew 4:10).

Even the drawing of this initial is far from complete, in places only sketched in outline. The drapery patterning, so often elaborately drawn out in these designs, is here only indicated, although it is certain that the hem of St Mark's garment would have been of gold.

St Luke, f.395

The gospel of St Luke opens with the events leading up to the Nativity, starting with the birth of John the Baptist to Zacharias and Elizabeth. The initial 'Q', QUONIAM QUIDEM, depicts the angel's revelation to Zacharias: 'Fear not, Zachary, for thy prayer is heard; and thy wife Elizabeth shall bear thee a son. And thou shalt call his name John.' (Luke 1:13). The design is complete, with the robes and the trappings of the Temple picked out in gold. The terminal of the 'Q', inserting itself into the text of the right-hand column, provides a perfect example of the close working between the scribe, who left a small gap, and the designer, who filled it.

St John, f.407

The establishment of Christ as the Son of God is the main theme of the first chapter of the Gospel of St John, as the Evangelist quotes John the Baptist's restatement of the prophecies of the Old Testament, and identifies Christ, 'and I gave testimony that this is the Son of God' (John 1:34). And the opening of the gospel text echoes the start of Genesis, IN PRINCIPIO, reminding the reader of the time of Creation, 'In the beginning was the Word and the Word was with God and the word was God' (1:1), equating the Word with Christ, Son of God. The opening initial presents this clearly, with the enthroned Christ at the top, the evangelist John in the centre, his eagle-headed body flanked with wings, and at the base the Virgin enthroned with the Child. The frame of the initial and the hems of the garments are gilded, the whole ready for painting.

The Acts of the Apostles, f.417v

Acts follows the events after the death and resurrection of Christ, his Ascension, and Pentecost: 'And suddenly there came a sound from heaven, as of a mighty wind coming; and . . . there appeared to them parted tongues, as it were of fire . . . and they were all filled with the Holy Ghost . . .' (Acts 2:2–4). The text begins with a huge space, 416×120mm. ($16\frac{1}{3} \times 5$ins) in size, for the 'P', PRIMUM QUIDEM SERMONEM. The display letters are complete, shaped around the absent initial, and instructions in the margin tell the illuminator to supply the two opening scenes, the Ascension and the Pentecost.

The Epistles, ff.428v–63, figs. 25 and 73

The Epistles held a position of great importance in the bible of the Middle Ages. Where the Gospels were considered as a parallel to the Old Testament narratives of the Law, from Genesis to Deuteronomy, the Epistles, written by the apostles of Christ, were considered to be a parallel to the books of the prophets. The teaching of the early church, set out in the epistles, provided texts for medieval teachers, and for the liturgy, with a selection from the epistles for each day's celebration of the Mass.

Whether St Jerome revised the Epistles for the Vulgate is not certain. His revision of the Gospels is well documented, but although he talks of his work on the 'New Testament', implying the whole text including the Epistles, when St Augustine speaks of Jerome's New Testament revisions he speaks exclusively of the Gospels. Even so, many of these epistles are prefixed by a prologue, ascribed to St Jerome, and

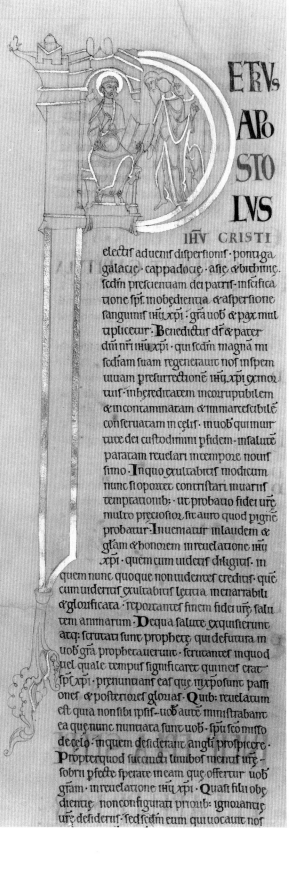

73 The Epistle of St Peter (f.430v), *unfinished, Master of the Leaping Figures*

most, in addition to a full capitula list, include the *argumentum*.

None of the Epistles has a finished illuminated initial, yet there are thirteen which have fully drawn out designs, some gilded ready for painting. The richness of these initials lies chiefly in their elaborate decoration, and the historiated few depict the letter-writer disseminating his words. The Epistle of St James (f.429) opens, 'James, the servant of God and of our Lord Jesus Christ, to the twelve tribes which are scattered abroad, greeting.' (James 1:1), and the initial, simply pen-drawn, shows the author perched high on a tower, casting down his scroll to figures in its base. St Peter also sends out his words. On f.430v at the start of his first Epistle, he is seated within a niche, his key over his shoulder, passing a bound codex to three messengers eager to depart. Like an address, the Epistle begins: 'Peter, an apostle of Jesus Christ, to the strangers dispersed through Pontus, Galatia, Cappadocia, Asia and Bithynia . . .' (Peter 1:1). Here the gold is applied, defining the curve of the 'P', but the display script is set as a vertical column, unlike its encirclement of the empty space for the initial to Acts.

Frivolity dominates the initial 'P' to the prologue to the Pauline Epistles (f.435), the Epistle to Philomones, filled with a vine-scroll inhabited by a truly leaping figure (f.459), that to the Phillipi occupied by a splendid stork (f.452v), and the Epistle to Timothy which starts with a somersaulting lion (f.456v). In contrast, the Epistle to Titus (f.458v) opens with a solemn portrait bust of St Paul, a book in one hand, his finger raised in instruction in keeping with the serious task he sets Titus, 'For this cause I left thee in Crete; that thou shouldest set in order the things that are wanting and shouldest ordain priests in every city, as I also appointed thee.' (Titus 1:5).

The final Epistle is to the Hebrews, on f.460v, marked only by a space. The final book of the Bible, the Apocalypse, similarly opens in iconographic silence.

Apocalypse, f.463v, fig.74

The Apocalypse, the Book of Revelation, remains a prophecy to be fulfilled: 'The Revelation of Jesus Christ which God gave unto him, to make known to his servants, the things which must shortly come to pass'. Sent to 'his servant John' (Apocalypse 1:1), the Apocalypse confirms the unity of Christ and God, and rounds off the New Law in the context of the Old: 'I am Alpha and Omega, the beginning and the end, saith the lord God, who is and who was and who is to come, the Almighty' (1:8). Full of prophecies and portents, of visions and apparitions – the book with seven seals opened by the Lamb, the angels with

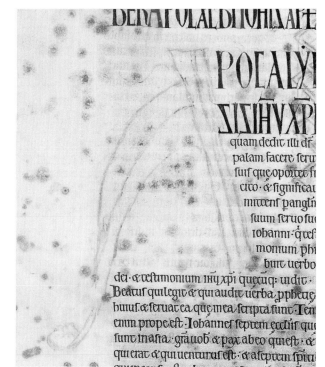

74 The Book of Revelation, the Apocalypse, f.463v, *unfinished*

trumpets, the army of horsemen, the woman clothed with the sun and the great whore of Babylon – the imagery is rich like the prophecies of the Old Testament, yet relevant to Christian man and quoted constantly in the liturgy. The judgements of God are concluded by the prophecy of the Last Judgement, an ubiquitous image in the Middle Ages. And the new Jerusalem of Chapter 21 draws the sweetness out of the 'pool of fire': 'And I saw a new heaven and a new earth . . . and I, John, saw the holy city the new Jerusalem, coming down out of heaven from God, prepared as a bride adorned for her husband. . . And God shall wipe away all tears from their eyes; and death shall be no more; nor mourning, nor crying, nor sorrow shall be any more; for the former things are passed away' (21:1–4).

The initial is marked out in red chalk, but the instruction for the illuminator survives at the base of the page. It is a small space to encompass the imagery of this final text. Ending the Apocalypse is one further avowal of the truth of the scriptures, an epilogue for the Bible itself, and for this short exploration of the Winchester Bible:

'For I testify . . . if any man shall take away from the words of the book of this prophecy, God shall take away his part out of the book of life . . . and from these things that are written in this book.' (Apocalypse 22:18–19).

FURTHER READING

This study has looked at the Winchester Bible in three ways: as a possession of a bishop and the community of monks which served his cathedral, as an example of the Vulgate as used in the Middle Ages, and as a fine illuminated manuscript which reveals the processes by which it was made and the artists who designed and illustrated it. These suggestions for further reading therefore follow up those three strands.

A new volume on many aspects of the Cathedral to commemorate 900 years since the consecration in 1093, *Winchester Cathedral – Nine Hundred Years*, is edited by John Crook, and published by the Dean and Chapter of Winchester Cathedral with Phillimore and Co., 1993.

For the history of the monastic setting of the Bible, see D. Knowles, *The Monastic Order in England, 940–1216* (Cambridge, 1940; 2nd ed. 1963); Colin Platt, *The Abbeys and Priories of Medieval England* (London, 1984); and J. A. Lamb, 'The place of the bible in the liturgy', in *The Cambridge History of the Bible*, edited by P. R. Ackroyd and C. F. Evans (Cambridge, 1970), pp. 563–87. Specialist articles on medieval Winchester are found in *Medieval Art and Architecture at Winchester Cathedral*, British Archaeological Association (1983).

For Bishop Henry of Blois, see Chapter 16 in Knowles, *Monastic Order*; G. Zarnecki, 'Henry of Blois as a patron of sculpture', in *Art and Patronage in the English Romanesque*, edited by Sarah Macready and F. H. Thompson (London, 1986), pp. 159–72; Yoshio Kusaba, 'Henry of Blois, Winchester and the Twelfth-century Renaissance', in *Winchester Cathedral – Nine Hundred Years*.

For the Vulgate and St Jerome, see H. H. Glunz, *History of the Vulgate in England* (Cambridge, 1933); H. F. D. Sparks, 'Jerome as a biblical scholar', in *The Cambridge History of the Bible*, pp. 510–41; J. N. D. Kelly, *Jerome, his life, writings and controversies* (London, 1975).

For the Winchester Bible, see W. Oakeshott, *The Artists of the Winchester Bible* (London, 1945); W. Oakeshott, *The Two Winchester Bibles* (Oxford, 1981), and C. M. Kauffmann, *Romanesque Manuscripts, 1066–1190* (London, 1975), no. 83. See also my chapter, 'The Winchester Bible', in *Winchester Cathedral – Nine Hundred Years*. Specialist articles include L. M. Ayres, 'The Work of the Morgan Master at Winchester and English painting of the early Gothic period', *Art Bulletin*, 56, 1974, pp. 201–23.

For medieval manuscripts and art, see Christopher de Hamel, *A History of Illuminated Manuscripts* (Oxford, 1986), and the same author's *Medieval Craftsmen Scribes & Illuminators* (London, 1992); Jonathan J. G. Alexander, *Medieval Illuminators and their Methods of Work* (London and New Haven, 1993); *English Romanesque Art 1066–1200*, edited by George Zarnecki, Janet Holt and Tristram Holland (London, 1984); W. Oakeshott, *Sigena: Romanesque paintings in Spain and the Winchester Bible artists* (London, 1972); David Park, 'The wall paintings in the Holy Sepulchre Chapel,' in *Winchester Cathedral* (BAA, 1983).

GLOSSARY

bifolium parchment folded to form two folios, sewn into binding

canon tables concordance tables to Gospels, showing parallel passages, usually set out in columns beneath decorative arches

capitulae chapter headings listed at start of each biblical book, as contents list

Chapter daily meetings of the community to transact business and receive instruction, held in the chapter house

damp-fold method of depicting drapery, mostly Romanesque, to reveal contours of body, and particularly movement, through thin fabrics clinging to the form, as if damp

display lettering large letters in colour at beginning of text, including rubrics and usually the first verse

foliation numbering of folios; each folio has recto and verso face

illumination embellishment of a text using gold leaf
   illuminator designer and painter of decorative and pictorial work

initial first letter of text
   historiated pictorial, containing illustrative story
   illuminated with gilding, may also be historiated
   painted decorative in two or three colours, with brush, or quill

miniature framed picture, separate from text

Mosan describes a centre of production, 11–13th centuries, centred on the Meuse River valley, particularly famed for metalwork and enamel

rubric title or instruction at start of new text, often in red
   incipit rubric identifying start of text
   explicit rubric identifying end of text
   rubricator scribe who adds the rubrics

quire gathering of leaves, folded down the centre for binding. The quires in the Winchester Bible comprise four *bifolia*, folded to form gatherings of 8 leaves (folios)

parchment animal skin, mostly sheep or calf, prepared as a writing surface; sometimes called 'vellum'

Romanesque style prevalent in Europe at its most characteristic during the twelfth century, robust and solemn in its buildings, dynamic and expressive in its depiction of figures

Vulgate the Latin bible as used throughout the Western church, chiefly derived from the translations of St Jerome (342–420); see pp. 11–13